Open Canoe Technique

John and Rachel
October 1998

Open Canoe Technique

A complete guide to paddling the open canoe

Nigel Foster

fernhurst
B O O K S

First published 1996 by Fernhurst Books,
Duke's Path, High Street, Arundel, West Sussex,
BN18 9AJ, UK. Tel: 01903 882277.

Printed and bound in Great Britain

British Library Cataloguing in Publication Data:
A catalogue record for this book is available
from the British Library.

ISBN 1 898660 26 3

Acknowledgments
The author and publisher would like to thank
Dagger Canoe Company and Mobile Adventure
Ltd for their assistance in preparing this book
and for the loan of the boats and equipment
featured in the photographs. The author would
also like to thank Jos Ribbens, Trys Morris and
John Tribe.

Photographic Credits
Cover photo of the Emery River, Nemo TN by
Robert Harrison, courtesy of Dagger.
Location shots of Nigel Foster in action by
Simon Jackson and Linda Schuster.
Sailing canoe photos courtesy of John Bull,
Solway Dory, Carlisle. Other photos courtesy of
Dagger Canoe Company.

Edited by Jean McLean

Cover design by Simon Balley

DTP by Creative Byte

Printed and bound by
Hillman Printers, Frome

Other books by Nigel Foster

Sea Kayaking (Fernhurst Books)
Canoeing: A Beginner's Guide to the Kayak
(Fernhurst Books)
Raging Rivers Stormy Seas (with Storrie &
Baillie) (Oxford Illustrated Press)
British Canoe Union Handbook (the chapter
on Sea Kayaking)

To my father, Peter,
who first introduced me to
the delights of paddling.

The author in action.

Contents

1 What you will need

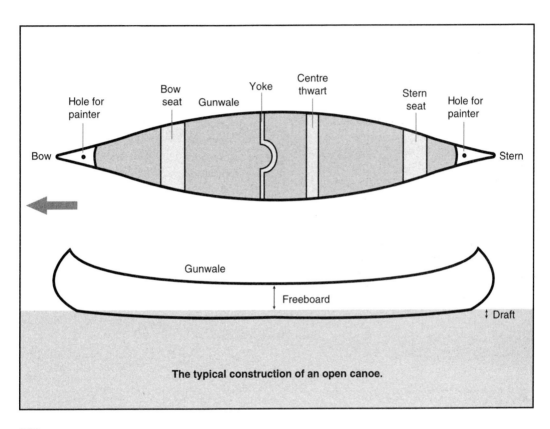

The typical construction of an open canoe.

The canoe

The traditional canoe is one of the most versatile open-topped watercraft. It is well suited to load carrying and can be paddled either solo or with companions. Because it is so easily carried and readily car-topped, it makes an ideal recreational craft. Most paddlers use the canoe for gentle water cruising, but skilled paddlers in specialist craft can negotiate serious white water, or make wilderness expeditions. The craft I will be describing in this chapter is a steady 'middle of the road' canoe suitable for cruising and for gentle white water.

A canoe should have a gunwale (gunnel), thwarts, seats, and fixed buoyancy. The gunwale is the structural strip around the top of the hull defining the open deck. The thwarts are gunwale-to-gunwale strengthening bars that hold the two sides of the hull apart at the top against the pressure of the water. Canoes outfitted for white water generally have extra thwarts to cope with the additional stresses. Although thwarts are not designed for sitting on, they are often used as a bar to brace against while kneeling on the floor when an alternative paddling position is required. Seats are obviously for sitting on.

Inside a white-water canoe.

A canoe with a symmetrical hull will move through the water equally efficiently in either direction. One of the two seats is usually closer to an end than the other. Use this as the rear seat when you paddle tandem. Paddling solo, face in the opposite direction and use the seat so that your weight is more central.

With an asymmetrical canoe, the hull is shaped for better forward efficiency through the water, but will not perform so well in reverse. It should always be paddled with the same end being used as the bow. For this reason, asymmetrical canoes are normally fitted with an additional seat near the centre for solo paddling.

Buoyancy is essential. There should be sufficient flotation to prevent your canoe from sinking completely if you swamp, and also to help you keep afloat following a swamping. But a buoyant canoe is more easily self-rescued, and more easily swum back to shore, so any extra buoyancy beyond the minimum can only help you. Consider securing extra airbags in the bow and stern and/or in the centre of the canoe.

The paddle

A basic general purpose paddle has a straight shaft, a flat blade and some form of hand grip. The length of the paddle depends on your height above the water when you are sitting in your canoe. This is tricky to determine because different seats and canoes place you at different heights above the water. The whole paddle blade needs to be just immersed during paddling, irrespective of the length of the blade, so it is only the shaft length that needs to be tailored to you. As a rough guide, sit on your canoe seat with your arm outstretched in front of you at shoulder height, holding the hand grip so that the paddle hangs vertically down into the water. If the whole of the blade is now just immersed, the paddle length is reasonable for you.

An alternative way of measuring is to sit on a chair and measure from your chin to the chair seat. Add this measurement to the height of the canoe seat above water level. This again gives you a rough guide to the shaft length, not the overall length, of the paddle.

Buoyancy aid
(Personal Flotation Device or PFD)

A buoyancy aid is a jacket designed to help you float in water. When you are afloat, it should be worn at all times. The International Canoe Federation recommends that there should be a minimum of 13 pounds (6 kilograms) of inherent buoyancy. The most common design is a waistcoat-shaped jacket with panels of soft buoyant foam in the front and back. It is either pulled over your head like a sweater or put on like a jacket. It should then be fastened securely at the front and around the waist to prevent the jacket from riding up your body when you are in the water.

Your chosen P.F.D. should be a good fit, not too loose or too tight, and should be fitted and worn according to the manufacturer's recommendations. It must be comfortable to wear in use. Check your arms for freedom of movement. Can you extend both arms straight

in front of you without being restricted by the foam at your chest? Can you windmill your arms without restriction to your armpits? Can you breathe without difficulty? Check for possible chafe points and make sure that the jacket will fasten sufficiently well to prevent it riding up around your face when you are in the water.

The foam used in most buoyancy aids deteriorates with age, gradually losing buoyancy, and the outer shell fabric also degrades. Simple care will maximize its useful life. Compression damages foam, so avoid sitting on your buoyancy aid or resting heavy objects on it. Sunlight, excessive heat and water pollutants are the other main causes of rapid deterioration. Ideally, rinse your buoyancy aid in fresh water after each use, hang it up to dry, and store indoors by hanging away from direct sunlight or excessive heat.

Clothing

Paddling clothing must take into account both the weather and the possibility of a swim. In hot weather consider the effects of the sun even when cloudy. You burn much more readily on water, where you are subjected to reflected light, than on land. Try wearing a long-sleeved garment, a brimmed or peaked hat and, because your legs will be vulnerable to burning in the sitting position, some leg covering together with footwear and your buoyancy aid. Sunglasses will protect your eyes against glare. Secure them to your buoyancy aid or to a floating head-strap to prevent loss in water.

In cold weather wear a complete layer of wool or thermal fleece with a wind and waterproof outer layer, wool socks inside your footwear, plus your buoyancy aid and a wool hat. Alternatives include a neoprene wetsuit that allows sufficient freedom of arm movement, or a dry suit over warm fleece or wool. These are

Your PFD should be a good fit and be worn according to the manufacturer's instructions whenever you are on the water.

especially good when the chances of capsize are significant, such as on white water.

Footwear should protect against sharp objects underfoot, particularly in the water where they may not be seen, but must not hinder your swimming. Training shoes, lightweight close-fitting Wellington boots or neoprene watersports boots are fine. Wear wool socks inside for extra warmth.

Bailers

You need a bailer. A plastic dustpan does the trick remarkably well. A sponge gets the last drops out but cannot cope with the quick removal of any great quantity of water. Bailers should be clipped to the canoe with elastic or line and a simple plastic clip to prevent loss in a capsize. It is sometimes difficult to use a bailer if your canoe is fitted with saddle seats. Then use a stirrup pump.

2 Preparing to go afloat

Calm, non-moving water is best for your first attempts at paddling.

Where to paddle

Look for fairly calm, non-moving water with an easy shore for launching and landing. At first choose an enclosed body of water such as a pond or small lake, where you are always near to a shore. If there is a breeze, launch from a shore into the breeze so that you will be blown back to shore if you find things difficult. Until you have gained a degree of control, avoid places with swimmers, powerboats or anglers' lines. For your first excursions at least, try to go with an experienced paddler: two boats are always better for safety than one. Otherwise, use common sense and have a companion on the shore who is capable of helping if needed, and stay near the shore. For more detailed safety considerations refer to chapter 19.

Picking up a canoe. Stand beside the canoe facing the stern. Grasp the gunwale each side, just forward of the yoke.

Roll the canoe onto its side.

Settle the yoke onto your shoulders.

Carrying a canoe

Solo carrying requires the most technique. If your canoe is fitted with a carrying yoke, this should indicate the balance point. Stand beside the centre of the canoe, facing the stern. Reach across and grasp the gunwale at each side of the canoe just forward of the yoke. You should still be facing the stern. Roll the canoe towards you onto its side then, resting the stern on the ground, raise the canoe over your head. Pivot to face the bow. Gently settle the carrying yoke

Setting a canoe down. Ease the stern onto the ground.

Lift the yoke from your shoulders, turn sideways and roll the canoe onto its side.

Pivot to face the bow.

Lean forward to balance the canoe.

onto your shoulders. Lean forwards to raise the stern and bring the canoe level. Keep your grip on the gunwales in front of you, elbows bent at right angles beneath your hands. Carrying the canoe in this position is surprisingly easy, but remember to raise the bow slightly to see

Pivot to face the stern as you bring the canoe to the ground.

where you are going.

To set the canoe back down, first lean backwards slightly to rest the stern on the ground. Lift the yoke from your shoulders, turn towards the side on which you wish to place the canoe and roll it slowly onto its side. Turn to face the stern as you bring the canoe onto the ground.

In the absence of a carrying yoke, a centrally-positioned thwart or seat may be used. Alternatively an improvised yoke can be rigged by tying a paddle across the gunwales, the line passing around the hull.

Tandem, either simultaneously lift the canoe into position in a similar manner to the solo technique, or raise one end for the first person to get into position, after which the second can duck into place. It helps if the taller person goes at the front so that you can see where you are going. Carrying is then no great problem except in strong winds.

Carrying the canoe under-arm from opposite ends and sides to your partner is a good alternative. But be careful: you can twist your back if the canoe is heavy. More people can assist. Check the security of your chosen lifting point. Note that the small triangular decks at the bow and stern may not be strong enough: gunwales and thwarts are usually best if the manufacturer has not built in special handles.

A trolley will make carrying a lot easier providing the ground is suitable. There are several good models on the market that will stow in one piece in the canoe while you paddle, or which can be dismantled for easier packing.

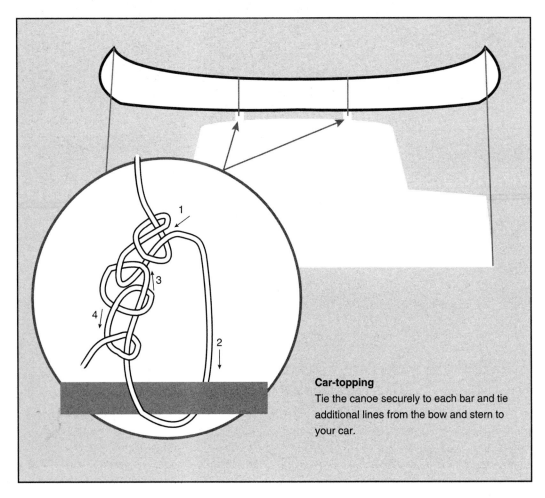

Car-topping

Tie the canoe securely to each bar and tie additional lines from the bow and stern to your car.

Car-topping

Canoes are regularly carried on car roof bars but there are a few points to consider. Check the weight of the canoe against the maximum roof load for your vehicle and the maximum loading for your roofrack. The basic roofrack system with two bars is generally sufficient, although you may wish to pad the bars to protect your canoe and to prevent it sliding. The further apart you can place the bars, up to about two-thirds of the total length of the canoe, the better for security. Use straps designed for load strapping or sturdy rope to tie the canoe to each bar, then tie additional lines to the front and back of your car from the bow and stern. The

extra lines from the bow and stern should prevent the canoe from leaving the roof in the event of an emergency stop or a traffic accident, when roof bars have been known to slide along the roof, shear or even tear free. Extra care could prevent someone getting your canoe through their windscreen. The extra ties also make the canoe less likely to shift in winds.

On a legal point, check your local laws and regulations regarding the carrying of loads. There may be restrictions on the length of canoe you are permitted to carry on your car, the length of overhang allowed at the front or back, or the requirement for a red flag, triangle, or lighting board. Check it out and be safe!

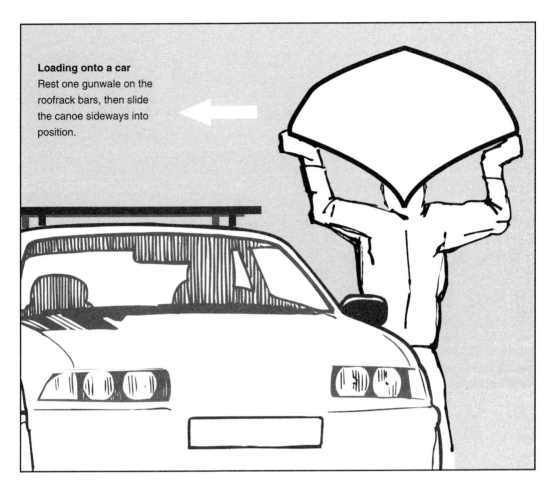

Loading onto a car
Rest one gunwale on the
roofrack bars, then slide
the canoe sideways into
position.

Loading onto a car

Carrying a canoe using a yoke is the easiest
approach to a standard car for loading. Simply
walk alongside the car with the canoe on your
shoulders, rest one gunwale on the ends of the
roofrack bars, grip the other gunwale with both
hands and slide the whole canoe sideways onto
the rack. Lifting the canoe off again is similarly
straightforward. Slide the canoe partly off the
rack to the side, then step underneath into the
carrying yoke before sliding the final gunwale
from the rack. Taller vehicles can be more
awkward to load. One solution is to install a third
bar at one end of the roof with a length of tube to
act as a roller. Once one end has been lifted
onto this roller, the canoe can be pushed

forward and lowered onto the other two bars for
tying. Another interesting system fastens to the
ball hitch of a vehicle. One end of the canoe is
lifted and secured onto the swivel before the
other end is lifted and brought around to rest on
the front bar of the rack. The swivel is then
lowered until the canoe also rests on the rear
bar of the rack.

Which way up should you transport the canoe?
A lot will depend on the weather and how far
you need to travel. In heavy rain, an excessive
weight of water will soon collect in an upright
canoe. However, when you carry your canoe
inverted, make sure it does not block your
view for driving.

Full sitting position

Seating positions for paddling

When you paddle there is a tendency to slide
forwards in the canoe unless you are braced in
some way. There are several different sitting
and kneeling positions you can adopt. Some
offer better bracing potential than others, but all
have applications. Familiarise yourself with them
all so that, when you need to, you can change.

Sitting

Sit on your seat with your feet resting apart, flat
on the floor. This is the relaxing position
adopted for a switching style of paddling (see
later in this chapter). If you find your knees get
in the way of your paddle when you recover the
blade from the water, extend your legs further
forward. Your centre of gravity is quite high in
this position, so when moving into areas of
rougher water, drop one or both knees into one
of the kneeling positions described below.

Half-kneeling

This is an excellent cruising position for use with
a J-stroke (see later in this chapter) or one of the
other 'paddle and steer' strokes. Sit upright on
your seat. If you intend to paddle on the right,
tuck your right foot under your seat. If you
intend to paddle on the left then tuck your left
foot under the seat. Extend your other leg
forward to brace your foot against the side of the
hull, knee slightly bent. This is the bracing
position I feel most comfortable with for any
distance and it also provides tight enough
control for manoeuvring.

Full-kneeling

Sit on the front of your seat with your feet tucked
under the seat and your knees spread on the
floor. This position gives you a low centre of
gravity for added control on rough water and for
tight manoeuvring.

Half-kneeling position

Other kneeling positions

In the positions described above you are sitting with most, if not all, of your weight on a seat. In addition there are true kneeling positions where your weight is fully on your knees. Kneel upright (thighs vertical) immediately behind a thwart, knees spread and with your thighs resting against the thwart. Alternatively, kneel upright immediately in front of a thwart with your buttocks resting against the thwart.

Full-kneeling position.

High kneeling.

For a lower centre of gravity, kneel with both knees on the floor, the soles of your feet upright and your buttocks resting on your heels. This position may be used anywhere along the length of the canoe, although with high-sided canoes you may need to sit close to the side and tilt the canoe in order to reach the water comfortably. Switching then becomes impractical.

FORWARD PADDLING

Holding the paddle

Hold the paddle vertically in front of you with the blade down. Grasp the hand grip in one hand and the shaft in the other. The palm of your top hand should rest on top of the hand grip, with your fingers lightly wrapped around it. Your bottom hand should hold the shaft, thumb uppermost. The flat of the blade needs to be facing you. Now swing the paddle into a horizontal position across your chest and move your bottom hand along the shaft until your hands are about shoulder width apart.

The basic forward stroke

To practice the paddle movement before going afloat, sit upright in a tall chair, holding your paddle as described above, but with your left hand on the hand grip (your top hand) and your right hand on the shaft (your bottom hand). Now move your feet so that they rest flat on the floor about eighteen inches (0.5 metres) apart with your knees bent at right angles. Power for forward paddling comes from rotation of the torso with the arms held fairly straight, rather than from pulling with the arms. Extend your arms so that the paddle is upright in front of you and to the right of your right foot. Keep your body upright, don't lean to one side. Now raise the paddle, keeping both arms straight, and rotate your upper body to the left. Your right

Holding the paddle for the forward stroke.

The basic forward stroke. The forward paddle stroke begins with a smooth rotation of the torso guiding the blade down.

Keeping both arms straight throughout, pull back past your right foot and almost as far as your hip.

arm should now be horizontal, with your right hand somewhere above your left knee. The forward paddle stroke begins here with a smooth rotation of the torso guiding the blade down, then back past your right foot and almost as far as your hip. Keep both arms straight throughout, your left arm no lower than shoulder height. The power component of the forward stroke ends when your blade reaches your hip.

Now swing your left arm left across your body, thumb angling forwards while you lift the paddle with your right hand, your right elbow rising high. The effect should be to guide the paddle blade forwards, edge first, while also raising it.

Now rotate your torso fully around into your starting position once more. The whole action is rather like the coiling and uncoiling of a spring: you coil forwards ready to begin the stroke and you uncoil your body throughout the power part of the stroke.

Try linking your breathing with the action. Breathe out with the coiling and in with the uncoiling. Paddling should become smooth, rhythmic and pleasant!

Now switch hands and practice the same movement on the left side. You should aim to become equally fluent on both sides with all

The power component of the forward stroke ends when your blade reaches your hip.

turning effect. This seldom works perfectly though, and there is usually a need for steering even when paddling tandem.

Switching

Switching is normally done every few strokes in order to keep the canoe tracking straight. It is an efficient way of keeping straight and the method chosen in marathon racing, as well as all paddling where bent-shafted paddles are used. At the end of your paddle stroke slide your bottom hand up the shaft to the top hand as you lift the paddle out of the water. Bring your top hand off the hand grip and onto the paddle shaft. Adjust your grip swiftly while the paddle is in the air and bring the blade smoothly into the water on the opposite side.

The J stroke

The J stroke (you can see photographs in chapter 4) is probably the most universally known of a range of forward paddling strokes which incorporate a steering component. At the end of the basic forward stroke rotate the blade through ninety degrees by simultaneously turning both hands: turn the thumb of the top hand to point down at the water and cup the bottom hand, palm uppermost. This directs the power face of the blade (the face towards you when you began the stroke) outwards from the canoe. Continue to guide the paddle back until the forearm of your rear hand is vertical (elbow above hand) then lever gently across the canoe with your front hand until you have adjusted your direction sufficiently. Slice the blade out and return to the starting position for your next stroke. Note that with this stroke you always use the same face of your blade for power.

your paddling strokes.

The steering component of the forward stroke

Paddling on only one side of the canoe will make the canoe turn constantly towards the other side. Canoeists overcome this by either performing the basic forward stroke described above but switching sides every few strokes, or by adding a steering component to the forward stroke and paddling mostly on one side. Alternatively they team up with a partner who paddles on the opposite side to counteract the

3 Getting in and out

Launching

To prevent damage, make sure your canoe is afloat before you get in it. Lay your paddle in the canoe or across the gunwales where you will be able to reach it easily from your seat. Grasp the nearest gunwale or thwart a little forward of the seat and pull the canoe firmly towards you. Still pulling the canoe close, crouch and place one foot on the centreline of the canoe (halfway across from side to side) just in front of the seat. Transfer your weight onto the canoe and sit down on your seat. Now bring your second foot aboard and take up your paddle.

Landing

To get out again, come to shore (shallow water, bank or jetty), stow your paddle in the canoe and grasp the gunwale at either side in front of you. Crouch forward off the seat with one foot on the centreline of the canoe and lift the other foot out onto the shore or into the shallow water. Shift your weight onto this foot while pulling the canoe towards it. When you step out with your other foot, keep a hold of the canoe to prevent it floating away. Land it by lifting one end and floating the canoe as far ashore as you can without dragging it on the ground, or tie it using a painter (a loose line attached to the bow or stern). In some situations it is simpler to lift one side and land the canoe sideways.

When landing against a jetty, hold the jetty with one hand. With the other hold the centre of the nearest thwart in front of you. Keep your weight in the centre of the canoe for balance.

Emptying the canoe

To empty a small quantity of water from the canoe you can use a bailer, pump or sponge.

Launching
Grasp the nearest gunwale or thwart a little forward of the seat and pull the canoe firmly towards you.

Still pulling the canoe close, crouch and place one foo on the centreline of the canoe.

Otherwise pull alongside a shallow bank or into a gently shelving beach and step out. Roll the canoe onto its side towards you by pulling on the far gunwale while pressing down on the near gunwale with your foot. This method will not work with a swamped canoe; even if you were strong enough to roll the canoe, you might damage it.

When handling a swamped canoe, always avoid lifting weight unnecessarily. Let the water support the canoe while you manoeuvre it or roll it over. Use your energy for lifting the canoe out of the water rather than lifting the water. Your choice of emptying technique for a waterlogged canoe will depend, in part, on the amount of flotation in the canoe. If it is fitted with

Transfer your weight onto the canoe and sit down on your seat.

Now bring your second foot aboard and take up your paddle.

Emptying your canoe
With the canoe alongside a shallow bank or a gently shelving beach, hold it as shown.

Pull on the far gunwale while pressing on the near gunwale with your foot.

a lot of buoyancy in the ends, roll it onto its side, raise one end and, when most of the water has drained out, turn it upside down to complete the job. Lift your end high before quickly flipping it upright to avoid scooping in more water.

If there is minimal buoyancy in the ends, you may find it easier to raise one end of the upright canoe. Keeping it raised, work your hands along one gunwale towards the centre of the canoe. The canoe will drain as you lift it. When you have reached the centre, float the canoe sideways onto the shore and roll it upside down to complete draining.

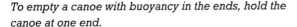

To empty a canoe with buoyancy in the ends, hold the canoe at one end.

Roll the canoe on its side.

Roll the canoe onto its side.

Raise one end and, when most of the water has drained out, turn it upside down to complete the

4 Forward paddling, stopping and reversing

Getting started

With a manoeuvrable canoe, your first paddle stroke may cause the boat to spin so much that the steering component of the J stroke will almost stop the canoe, leaving you where you started. Prevent this either by alternating sides for the first few strokes or by beginning your stroke with a bow draw (see chapter 7).

For alternating sides, maintain your normal hand grip on the paddle. Lift the paddle across to your offside (same hand on the grip) and place the blade in the water as far forward as you can comfortably reach. Rotate your torso to pull the blade back as far as your hip. Quickly change sides and perform a basic forward stroke on your nearside. Alternate sides for a few strokes until the canoe is moving forwards, then change your forward stroke on the nearside to a J stroke and paddle only on that side.

The alternative is to begin your forward stroke with a steering correction, pulling the bow sideways a little with a bow draw. The complete stroke, starting with a draw and continuing into a J stroke, is called a C stroke. This is a little more complicated than changing sides as described above, but should you wish to tackle it at this stage, read chapter 7 for instruction on draw strokes.

The J stroke. Keep your arms outstretched, with your hands about shoulder width apart. Place the paddle blade in the water close to the canoe as far forward as possible without leaning forwards.

Use torso rotation delivered through straight arms to provide the power. Continue the power phase of the stroke as far as the hip.

In-side means the side on which you are paddling.

Out-side means the opposite side to which you are paddling.

A cross stroke is one where you paddle briefly on the out-side without changing your grip on the paddle.

The J Stroke

(See chapter 2 for a dry land drill.)
Keep your arms outstretched, with your hands about shoulder width apart. Place the paddle blade in the water close to the canoe as far forward as you can reach without leaning forwards. Use torso rotation to provide the power, delivered through straight arms. Continue the power phase of the stroke only as far as the hip, then rotate the blade in the water, power face outwards. Begin the steering phase with the paddle shaft parallel to the canoe and the blade trailing. With your top hand just in front of your body lever the blade outwards to correct the canoe's course. Paddling should be

a smooth rhythmic movement. Try to make the blade enter and exit the water quietly and smoothly. Set yourself a target to aim at when practicing so that you can tell whether or not you are steering a straight course.

Paddling tandem, the paddler in the stern uses a J stroke while the bow paddler uses a straightforward paddle stroke. The steering component of the J stroke is ineffective from the bow position. If you are practicing tandem, change positions from bow to stern periodically so that you both get practice.

Reversing

There are three main ways of reversing solo: the backwater with cross back stroke, the reverse J, and the compound backstroke.

The backwater and cross back stroke

To carry out a backwater stroke rotate your torso to place the paddle in the water behind you, close beside the canoe. Straighten both arms and push the paddle forwards close to the

Rotate the blade in the water, power face outwards. Begin the steering phase with the paddle shaft parallel to the canoe and the blade trailing.

With your top hand just in front of your body lever the blade outwards to correct the canoe's course.

The backwater stroke. Rotate your torso to place the paddle in the water behind you, close beside the canoe.

side of the canoe. Using straight arms will allow full torso rotation and maximum power.

Paddling solo, do a backwater stroke on your nearside then, keeping the same hand grip, lift your blade across the canoe to place it in the water beside you on your offside. This time, the power face is towards the front of the canoe. Unwind your torso to pull on the paddle. You will not have a very long stroke on this side, but you can pull powerfully in this position, and can certainly counter any turn started by the stroke on the nearside. This is the cross back stroke. Alternate between the two sides to reverse, watching behind you to ensure that you keep on course and that your way is still clear.

Reversing tandem, steering corrections can be made by the bow paddler drawing or prying, (see chapter 7, Moving Sideways).

The reverse J

Begin your reversing stroke as with the backwater stroke, on the nearside. When the blade has passed through vertical in front of you, begin to rotate the blade as you extend it further away, until your top hand is close to your nearside shoulder and your bottom arm is fully extended. The blade rotates to present the power face of the blade towards the canoe. The palm of the nearside hand should face the front of the canoe. Your top hand should come into a position that would be ideal for reading a wristwatch on the back of the wrist. If you need additional steering, rest the paddle shaft against the gunwale in this position and lever the blade out from the side.

If you are doing a tandem reverse, only the bow paddler uses the steering component of this stroke. The stern paddler performs the backwater stroke described above.

Straighten both arms and push the paddle forwards close to the side of the canoe.

The compound backstroke

This is an addition to the backstroke that uses the power face of the blade. It is best visualized as a drawstroke performed from the stern, parallel to the canoe as far as the paddler's side, slicing back to the stern again with the power face towards the side of the canoe. Steering becomes easier when the canoe is pulled along in this way. This stroke may be combined with the simple backstroke, the second following the first after a roll of the blade to use the back of the blade for the second part of the stroke. This combination is the compound back stroke. Finish with a pry if necessary.

Stopping

To stop when you are paddling forwards, simply reverse or, when reversing, simply paddle forwards. You may need to make your first stroke on each side a little more gentle than subsequent strokes in order to lessen the strain on your arms, especially with a loaded canoe. However, when practicing, aim to stop the canoe with as few strokes and in as short a distance as possible. Practice with a soft floating object such as a partly filled plastic bottle. Aim straight at it then stop as rapidly as you can, keeping the canoe lined up with the target. Try using the backwater with cross back stroke and compare its effectiveness with that of the reverse J.

5 Canoe trim and balancing exercises

Canoe trim, fore and aft

The handling of a canoe is affected by where you place weight. If you weigh down the bow, it will sink deeper than the stern, causing the canoe to veer off course easily. On the other hand if the weight is too far back the stern will sink deeper than the bow. This will make tracking easier and the canoe will be much lighter to steer but there will be more drag (resistance to the water) so you will have to work harder and will travel more slowly.

The compromise is somewhere between the extremes, with the hull level in the water. This gives maximum waterline length, which is good for speed, and gives you the desired degree of tracking. Some paddlers prefer to move their weight back slightly to keep the bow just a little lighter in the water, aiding tracking without significantly affecting speed.

Canoe trim, side to side

Canoes are generally designed to be paddled upright. However it can sometimes be uncomfortable to solo paddle a broad canoe when you are in the middle of the centre seat. You can make a more comfortable and effective stroke by sitting closer to one side, but the canoe will then tilt. Paddling in this edged position has some enthusiastic followers, so is worth trying. Bear in mind that it precludes switching, so use a forward stroke with a steering component.

Paddling in an edged position. A more effective stroke may be made sitting closer to one side. In this edged position the canoe will sit with that gunwale closer to the water.

Trimming a canoe for wind

A central sitting position should result in your canoe resting comfortably across the wind but handling becomes more difficult when you try to turn and paddle into or away from the wind. If you move towards the bow, the canoe will point into the wind as the wind blows the lightened stern. If you move into the stern, the canoe will point downwind. By moving your weight forward or backwards it is possible to balance a canoe on any course in windy conditions; in this way the wind does the steering leaving your paddle stroke to provide the power - a very efficient way of paddling.

You can also trim the canoe to help you when you paddle tandem. It is worth finding the best balance point in a wind to save energy when keeping your course.

Trimming a canoe for wind. A central sitting position should result in your canoe resting comfortably across the wind.

If you move into the stern, your canoe will point downwind.

Trim for choppy conditions

When paddling into waves, lighten the bow a little by moving your weight back and you will ship less water, but beware of moving back too far or you will ship water over the sides near the stern. Paddling tandem into choppy water, try to keep both the bow and stern light and buoyant by moving closer together near the centre of the canoe.

Carrying a load

Canoes are excellent load carriers. They were once used as trading vessels, opening trade routes along the many North American river systems. You can make use of your load for trimming the canoe to your advantage.

By stowing your load up in the bow, you can sit closer to the stern. This is a more efficient paddling position because your paddle strokes are closer to the centreline of the canoe, requiring fewer course corrections. Moving cargo backwards or forwards in the canoe allows you to adjust the trim without the need to abandon the comfort of your seat for paddling.

Moving around in the canoe

If you intend to adjust the trim by changing your seating position or by moving your load, you must be confident moving around in the boat. Canoes are generally stable craft which rarely overturn without your help. There is a "safe" pathway along the centreline of the canoe. Keep to this when you move forward or back. Keep low. The higher you stand, the higher your centre of gravity is and the greater the risk of overbalancing. Keeping contact with both gunwales will help.

Turning around in a canoe is more tricky so reverse into your new position instead of turning around. When you do need to turn around, keep low and keep your weight over the centreline. Hold the gunwales while swivelling half way. Pause while you switch your hand position to opposite gunwales, then complete the swivel.

Try swapping positions with a partner while afloat. Stand, feet spread, hands gripping the gunwales, while your partner ducks below, keeping to the centreline of the canoe.

An alternative method is to pass your partner, facing one another in the centre of the canoe. Crouch low. This tends to be more tricky than the first method.

Swapping positions. Stand with your feet spread and your hands gripping the gunwales.

Keeping as low as possible, your partner ducks between your legs.

Balancing exercises to practice

- Move from one end seat to the other, turn round and move back. Hold the gunwales to help you balance. Keep to the centreline of the canoe.

- Stand in the centre of the canoe, feet spread by about twelve inches (30 cm). Gently transfer all your weight onto one foot, then onto the other. Now spread your feet a little at a time until they reach the sides of the canoe. Gently transfer as much of your weight onto one foot as you can, then bring your weight onto the other. Now bring your feet back into the centre. You should find the canoe balances best when you stand near the centreline.

- Taking small steps, walk towards one end of the canoe, keeping close to the centreline. As your weight depresses the end, the canoe will begin to slope up behind you. The closer to the end you go, the tippier the canoe will feel. Crouch down, turn around and stand up again facing the opposite direction. Now walk

to the other end of the canoe and repeat the exercise.

- Gunwale bobbing. Sit on the rear seat facing forward. Put your paddle across the canoe so that you can grip both the gunwales and the paddle just in front of you. Using your grip to help you balance, bring your feet up onto the gunwales to either side of the seat. Now stand, using the paddle in the manner of a tight-rope walker's pole. By bending your legs and crouching down and then straightening up abruptly you can alternately depress the stern into the water, then allow it to spring up again. The shape of the stern will cause the canoe to spring forward as the stern rises, propelling the canoe forwards.

  Experiment by moving a little further forwards or backwards until you find a standing position that is both comfortable for balance and effective for propulsion.

- Gunwale walking. Stand in your gunwale bobbing position. Brace your paddle against the angle between the centre thwart (or seat) and the gunwale while

Keeping to the centreline of the canoe, pass each other.

Still keeping low turn into your new positions.

holding the hand grip of the paddle. Push down on your paddle to keep the canoe balanced and walk gently along the opposite gunwale. When you reach the far end of your canoe, re-position your paddle on the opposite side and continue your gunwale tour back to where you started.

Practice is worthwhile

Balance and canoe trim are important, so it is worth spending time practicing moving around smoothly and experimenting with different seating positions in controlled conditions. Check the water for hazards before standing and moving around, remembering that the canoe will drift downwind. For more standing techniques, refer to chapter 17 on poling. If you intend to practice standing up in your canoe on open water, first study chapter 10 on rescues in deep water.

6 Turning

The forward sweep begins close to the bow with the blade on edge rather than on end. The power face should be outermost from the canoe.

Swivel the canoe by pushing forward on the near si(*with your knees and seat.*

The forward and reverse sweep

The further away from the canoe you make your forward or reverse paddle strokes the more your canoe will turn. The lower you hold the paddle shaft to the water, the further out you can reach with the blade. So to make effective turning strokes your paddle needs to be held low and swept wide. Keep your hand grip close to your body throughout.

The forward sweep

The forward sweep begins close to the bow with

The reverse sweep Rotate your torso towards the paddle and put the blade in the water at the stern.

Keep the hand grip close to your body.

Pull on the paddle so that it describes a wide arc from the turning canoe.

Lift the blade out on edge just before the blade meets the stern of the canoe.

the blade on edge rather than on end. The power face should be outermost from the canoe. Swivel the canoe by pushing forward on the near side with your knees and seat and pulling on the paddle so that it describes a wide arc from the turning canoe. Lift the blade out on edge just before the blade meets the stern of the canoe. Repeat. Try to put just sufficient pressure on the paddle to enable you to turn the canoe

without dragging the paddle through the water. If you are creating a lot of turbulence around the paddle, you are probably pulling too hard on it.

In some situations you may wish to start the stroke on the opposite side of the canoe. Cross your paddle over the canoe to the water straight out beside you on the offside. You will need to rotate your torso considerably. Keep your hand

Push the back of the blade out in a wide arc to the bow.

Remove the blade near the bow.

Doubles technique
When sweeping together to turn, the bow paddler performs a forward sweep to complement the rear paddler's reverse sweep on the opposite side.

grip close to your body and extend the blade from the canoe with the power face now facing forward. Sweep to the bow. Lift the paddle over the bow and continue the sweep on the nearside until the blade reaches the stern. In this way you will have described about three-quarters of a circle with the blade.

The reverse sweep

Rotate your torso towards the paddle and place the blade in the water at the stern, keeping the hand grip close to your body. Push the back of the blade out in a wide arc to the bow.

Doubles technique

The sweep stroke only works in full for the solo paddler. When turning tandem, the bow paddler normally uses only that part of the stroke forward of his seat, whilst the stern paddler uses only the part of the stroke that is behind his seat. When sweeping together to turn, the bow paddler performs a forward sweep to complement the rear paddler's reverse sweep on the opposite side, or alternatively the bow paddler sweeps in reverse while the rear paddler sweeps forward. The bow paddler can usefully use the segment of the sweep that is behind him to aid directional control in a wind. See chapter 7 for turning using a draw stroke.

7 Moving sideways

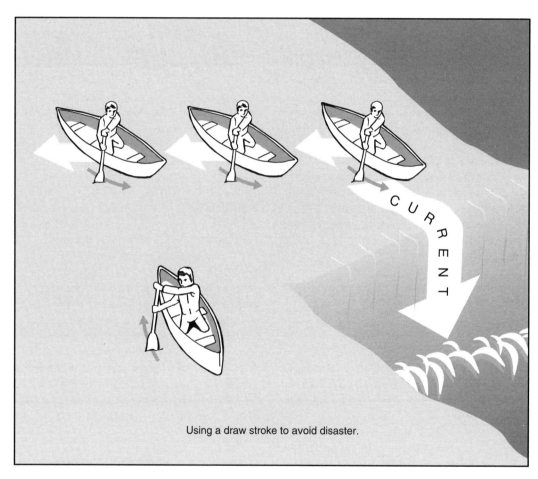

Using a draw stroke to avoid disaster.

The draw stroke

The basic stroke for moving sideways is called the draw stroke. Hold the paddle vertical in the water, about level with your hip. Rotate your torso towards the paddle. Reach out as far as you can to the side until both arms are nearly straight. The blade should be buried in the water with the power face towards the canoe.

This is the starting position for the draw stroke. Now pull towards you with your bottom hand while bracing away from you with your top hand. When the canoe meets the paddle blade, rotate the blade and slip it edge first back to the starting position. The power face should be toward the stern of the canoe during this recovery.

Drawing on opposite sides turns the canoe on the spot.

Repeat the stroke. The canoe should move sideways without turning. If it does turn, correct by moving both your starting and finishing points further forward or further back. If the stern is faster than the bow, move the draw stroke further in front of you. If this correction is ineffective, check that there is no pressure on either face of the blade when you slice it away to the starting position.

If you want the bow to move faster than the stern, use the same starting position but with the power face of the blade angled towards the bow. Draw towards the bow. This is a 'bow draw'.

If you want the stern to move sideways faster than the bow, angle the blade from the starting position towards the stern and draw towards the stern. This is a 'stern draw'.

Tandem, if the two paddlers draw on opposite sides, the canoe will turn on the spot. To draw the canoe straight sideways, you have several options. One paddler draws as normal, but the other may use a cross draw stroke, a pry, or a push away.

The cross draw

Keeping your normal hand grip, lift the paddle across the canoe to draw on the other side. The pulling phase of the draw stroke is similar to the standard draw stroke, but the slice away is achieved by turning the power face of the blade towards the bow of the canoe.

The pry

Place the paddle upright in the water beside you on the in-side of the canoe, with the power face against the hull. Your top hand should be extended out over the water with your bottom hand close above the gunwale. Use the gunwale as a fulcrum to lever the canoe away from the paddle by pulling with your top hand.

Rotate the blade edge-on, power face towards the stern, top hand extending out over the water once more to slice the blade back to the starting position. The stroke is short but powerful.

The push away

This is the true opposite of the draw stroke. The push away starts with the blade vertical in the water, with the power face against the hull beside you. Your top hand should be extended away further than the bottom hand. Push away on the paddle with your bottom hand while gripping the top hand firmly in position. Raise your hip on the opposite side to allow the canoe to slide sideways more easily. Slip the blade

back to the hull in the edge-on position, power face towards the stern, ready for a repeat stroke.

Sculling draw

Position your paddle with the blade vertical in the water beside you, top hand directly above the bottom hand. The power face should be towards you, with the blade just a little away from the side of the canoe. Before progressing to a sculling draw, practice slicing the blade forward about two feet (just over half a metre), then back behind you about the same distance, keeping on a line parallel to the side of the canoe. With your blade perfectly edge-on there should be no pressure on either side of the blade.

Now alter the angle of your blade so that the leading edge is a little further away from the canoe than the trailing edge. Try around forty five degrees from the side of the canoe to start with. As you guide the blade along parallel to the canoe, the canoe will draw sideways. Each time you change the direction of the paddle, rotate the blade until the new leading edge is angled away from the canoe. This is the sculling draw.

Now try sculling with the leading edge slightly closer to the canoe than the trailing edge in each direction. Your canoe will move away from your paddle. This is reverse sculling.

If you increase the angle of attack to much more than forty five degrees from the side, you will shunt the canoe forwards and backwards with little sideways movement. Reduce the angle too far and the blade will simply slip backwards and forwards through the water. Experiment with different angles between about ten and forty five degrees.

Tandem, you can use the sculling draw to turn the canoe, each paddler sculling on their own paddling side. You can also scull the canoe sideways, with one paddler sculling and the other reverse sculling.

Cross sculling

Cross your paddle to the out-side without changing your hand grip. Lock your arms relative to your body and scull using torso rotation. Compare the effectiveness of the cross scull with the reverse scull.

Tandem, one paddler cross sculls while the other sculls to draw the canoe sideways.

8 Draws on the move

Sideslip

The sideslip is basically a scull or cross scull but with the speed of the canoe through the water making it unnecessary for you to move the blade. Paddle forwards in a straight line. At the end of a forward stroke, when the blade reaches your hip, quickly turn the power face towards the canoe so that the blade slips through the water with minimum resistance, edge-on. Hold the paddle upright. Now rotate the paddle a bit more until the leading edge is further from the canoe than the trailing edge. The canoe should slip sideways without turning. If the bow turns to the paddle side, position your paddle a little further behind your hip next time. If the bow turns away from the paddle side, then next time position the paddle a little further forward. From a seating position behind the centre of the canoe you will probably need to position your paddle somewhere forward of your hip.

The sideslip can be performed on the outside of the canoe by reaching across and planting the paddle in a corresponding position, in the 'neutral' or edge-on position. The power face will be towards the side of the canoe. Now rotate the blade so that the leading edge is further from the canoe than the trailing edge.

When you have mastered the sideslip on both sides, try angling the blade so that the leading

Begin the cross bow rudder with the paddle out two or three feet (50 to 100 cm) from the side of the canoe.

'Pull' the bow round.

edge of the blade is closer to the canoe than the trailing edge. The canoe should sideslip away from the paddle.

Now try the whole range of paddle angles in reverse. Remember, for any reverse sideslip to work the canoe needs to be moving backwards.

Tandem, one paddler needs to do a standard sideslip while the other either uses a pushing angle on the blade or performs a cross sideslip.

RUDDERS

Sideslip at the stern

You can use the same sideslip at the stern to turn by pulling the stern sideways, or at the bow to turn towards the paddle. These are both important techniques for steering, turning and positioning. Generally the draw at

You must be moving forward for this steering rudder to work.

the bow is called a bow rudder, and the draw at the stern is called a stern draw (see chapter 7). These turns can usually be improved by edging the canoe away from the desired turn.

An alternative rapid turn

The paddle is thrust into the water close to the bow on the in- side. Retain a loose grip the paddle, allowing the water to push the blade against the hull, taking the angle of the hull. Water pressure will continue to press against the back of the blade pushing the bow rapidly sideways and turning the canoe towards the out-side. Anticipate the sudden turn and shift your weight towards the out-side of the boat for balance.

To turn towards the in-side, drop the paddle into the water close to the bow on your out-side. Retain a loose grip. Lean towards the inside of the turn for balance.

The bow rudder or bow cut

The bow rudder is basically a sideslip performed forward of the canoe's centre of turning. Begin the bow rudder with the paddle blade out two or three feet (50 to 100cm) from the side of the canoe. Plant the paddle in the required position rather than positioning it at the end of a forward stroke. As with the sideslip you will need to be moving forwards for this steering 'rudder' to work.

The cross bow rudder or cross bow cut

The cross bow rudder requires a similar paddle presentation but on the out-side of the canoe. Keep your hands in their normal grip when you cross over the canoe. The canoe should turn towards the out-side.

9 The paddle as a stabilizer

Braces

The brace makes use of the paddle as a stabilizer and provides a means of recovering your balance should you lose it.

The low brace

The low brace is used on the in-side of the canoe. The hand grip is held down close to the hip on the in-side and the blade extends out over the water at right angles to the side of the canoe. The back of the blade is presented to the water. The bottom hand is in a 'pushing down' position, elbow above but a little closer to the body than the hand. Keep your elbow bent.

The position of your head during a low brace

recovery is crucial. Your forehead needs to be low, close to your paddle shaft as you push up the canoe. If your head is high you will not get sufficient leverage from your body to flick the canoe upright.

Kneel with both knees on the floor, gripping the seat with your calves. Transfer your weight onto the in-side knee and buttock, unweighting your out-side buttock and lifting with the calf of your out-side leg. The canoe should lean towards the paddle but you may need to lean your body out over your paddle before it exceeds its balance point and starts to tip.

As soon as you feel the canoe lose its balance, lay the paddle flat on the water as described above and push down on it. Lift your in-side hip and knee and bring your forehead swiftly down towards the paddle-side gunwale by your hip. This action should snap the canoe sideways into position beneath your body, rather than pushing your body back over the canoe.

The offside brace

To recover from a loss of balance on your offside, use a draw stroke on your in-side. Push your top hand away and pull with your bottom hand. Lift sharply with your out-side buttock, knee and calf and throw your forehead towards your out-side shoulder.

Practice by leaning the canoe to its balance point on the out-side, then when the canoe finally exceeds its point of balance, recover with an offside brace.

Edging

The technique you have used to lean the canoe to its balance point is known as 'edging' and is used in moving water to aid stability when crossing eddy lines (see chapter 13). Try performing a low brace on the move. Keep the leading edge of the blade raised slightly so that the blade planes. While bracing, you should be able to hold the canoe comfortably at an angle as the canoe turns towards the paddle.

10 Open water rescues

Canoe over canoe rescue

Following a capsize you will have at least one paddler in the water waiting with the capsized canoe. Direct the swimmer to hold onto the gunwale of your canoe while you take hold of the swamped canoe. It is essential that the rescued person is holding on to your canoe before releasing his own. A canoe will float away across the water in the slightest breeze and will easily outstrip a swimmer. Failure to keep hold will make rescue considerably harder, if you want to keep control of the other canoe.

Either twist the canoe or roll it upright to break the air seal that may otherwise make it difficult for you to raise the canoe. Take hold of one end and draw it a few feet (about a metre) across the side of your canoe. If it is upright, invert it again now. Draw it across your gunwales until it is empty. Roll it upright and slide it back onto the water, bringing it tightly alongside your own canoe. Direct the capsized paddler(s) around to the far side of his canoe, where he can scramble aboard while you hold tightly to his near gunwale to steady it.

The rescue may be performed more quickly if the capsize victim(s) helps you lift the swamped

Canoe over canoe rescue

Approach the capsized canoe like this.

Twist or roll the canoe to break the air seal.

Roll the canoe upright.

Slide the canoe back onto the water.

Hold the canoes tightly, with the swimmer on the far side.

canoe across yours. As rescuer, tell the swimmer(s) what you would like them to do and where you want them to be. Make sure they retain a hold of either your canoe or their own at all times.

Self rescues

It is surprisingly easy to overbalance while moving around or poling, ending up in the water beside your empty canoe. Reach over the near gunwale and put both hands on the floor of the canoe close to you. Swim your legs up to the surface so that you are lying flat. Kick your legs and push the canoe down under your chest, keeping your head low. Aim to push it far enough to allow you to reach a point of balance. Now twist to sit in the bottom of the canoe and swing yourself aboard properly. Finally, pump or bail. An alternative that works well with canoes with low decks is to climb out onto the bow or stern deck by pushing it down and scrambling onto it as if you were climbing out of a swimming pool.

It is less common for both tandem paddlers to fall out of their canoe leaving it upright and empty, but re-entry is easier. One paddler steadies the canoe from the far gunwale while the other climbs in. The first to re-enter then stabilizes the canoe by keeping low while the second slides aboard.

With a swamped canoe the simplest option, if help is not at hand, is to roll the canoe upright, slide in as described for an empty canoe, hook your legs beneath a seat and either paddle or hand paddle back to shore to empty out. Bear in mind that it will be much slower paddling a swamped canoe than an empty one and that you will probably be floating up to your chest in water. Be aware of the risks of cold water and avoid paddling alone so that there is always at least one other canoe to perform a rescue if necessary. If all the canoes in your party capsize at the same time, swim the canoes together and empty one over the hull of another. Once one has been emptied and re-entered, that canoe can be used to empty the next and so on.

Draw the rescued canoe a few feet (about a metre) across the side of your canoe. If it is upright, invert it.

Draw the canoe across your gunwales until it is empty.

Roll the canoe on its side.

Tell him to scramble aboard.

Hold tightly to the near gunwale of the rescued canoe to steady it.

Steady the rescued canoe until the paddler is safely aboard.

Self rescue.
1. Pull yourself over the gunwale.
2. Reach over and put both your hands on the
floor. Kick your legs to the surface.
3. Push the canoe down under your chest.
4. Finally pivot and drop into the canoe with
your legs still over the side.
5. Pump or bail.

If you are landing through waves with a swamped canoe, climb out and swim it through to land from the offshore end of the canoe so that it cannot be carried against you by a wave. A swamped canoe is extremely heavy.

High-sided white water canoes can be very difficult to re-enter unaided, especially if well fitted with airbags.

Other ways of emptying canoes

There are a couple of other ways to empty a canoe while in the water. The Capistrano Flip relies on the swimming ability and coordination of the swimmer who lifts the canoe from underneath, throwing it up and over while kicking vigorously with his legs. This works best with more than one good swimmer and a lightweight boat.

Another technique is the shake-out, which involves the repeated shunting sideways of the canoe. Each shunt leaves some water behind and the remaining water in the canoe simply sloshes sideways and returns as a wave. The next shunt should coincide with the arrival of the wave, so that the water washes out over the gunwale, which is then raised again to prevent any water entering when the wave has passed. With skill and a canoe of the right shape, the canoe can be almost completely emptied in this way.

11 The open canoe roll

For efficient rolling your canoe should be well packed with buoyancy.

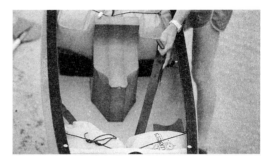

Fit out your canoe with a saddle-seat or central foam plinth with thigh straps, knee pads and foot braces.

Rolling

The roll is the ultimate form of self rescue for the canoeist. There are two levels of roll. One is a means of righting a canoe with minimal buoyancy, which is then paddled or hand paddled to shore for emptying. The other is a means of righting a canoe packed with buoyancy which can then be paddled adequately with a small amount of water remaining inside. For the first, it is adequate to hook your legs beneath the seat and to grip tightly while you roll the canoe up beneath you. The canoe will then be submerged or semi-submerged. For efficient rolling in a canoe well packed with buoyancy, fit out your canoe with a saddle-seat or central foam plinth, together with thigh straps, knee pads and foot braces.

Preparation

To prepare for rolling, practice low brace recovery strokes. Keep your top hand (grip hand) low in the water with your bottom hand (shaft hand) high. The paddle should extend at right angles to the canoe. Edge the canoe towards the paddle until you lose balance. Now bring the blade down onto the water. Your elbow should be bent above your paddle and the blade should be flat on the water. Twist your body, chest down, and drop your forehead towards the water. Keep your forehead close to the paddle shaft while you hook the canoe upright beneath you by bringing your hips sideways towards your head. Finally slide your head low across the gunwale towards the final balance point.

The roll. Arch your body out to your paddle side until you are close to the water surface, face down, and extend your blade out of the water at right angles to you.

Push against the blade. Keep your head down towards the paddle while pushing away with your offside knee and hip and pulling with your nearside knee and hip.

Jackknife your body, in-side hip towards your forehead, to bring the canoe upright beneath you. Finally slide your head aboard low over the gunwale to balance.

The roll

From an inverted position, arch your body out to your paddle side until you are as close as you can get to the water surface, but twisted face down. Bring the palm of your grip hand close to your chest and extend your blade out of the water at right angles to the canoe. Try to bring your elbow around into a pushing position above the paddle shaft while you are beneath it. If you cannot quite manage this, you will need to slide quickly into this position as soon as you begin your roll. Now push/brace against the blade. Keep your head down towards the paddle while pushing away with your offside knee and hip and pulling with your nearside knee and hip. Jackknife your body, in-side hip towards your forehead, to bring the canoe upright beneath you. Your forehead should still be down on the paddle. Finally slide your head aboard low over the gunwale to balance.

It is crucial that you use your body flick to right the canoe rather than pushing yourself up with your arms.

When practicing, concentrate on getting the back of the blade against the water, keeping your forehead close to the surface of the water throughout, and making a powerful body flick to bring the canoe up underneath you.

To keep the paddle blade on the surface, try sculling it across the water during the final stages of your roll. The back of the blade should sweep across in an arc reaching no closer forward or back than a forty five degree angle from the canoe. The leading edge of the blade should be slightly raised, giving the paddle the required lift. This is a useful way of completing your roll if the initial movement was not quite sufficient to bring you completely upright.

Safety considerations for rolling practice

- Have someone stand by in case you get into difficulty.

- Consider using a mask to help you see what you are doing to begin with, although ultimately you should be able to roll with your eyes shut.

- A nose clip will help prevent water getting into your sinus passages from repeated inversion.

- If the water is cold, it is prudent to protect your ears. Repeated rushes of cold water into the ears can lead to a condition commonly known as 'surfer's ear' (exostosis) in which the aural passage becomes restricted over time causing progressive deafness. It is a condition known amongst swimmers and surfers and some paddlers who spend a lot of time 'up to their ears' in cold water. A hat to cover the ears should do the trick.

- Always check the depth of water before practicing rolling, and be aware of your drift if there is a breeze.

- Cold water will chill you rapidly. Dress for the cold and finish your session before you get too cold. The onset of hypothermia may render you unable to make sensible decisions, so stop if you are shivering.

12 Moving water

Water tends to travel in straight lines unless its way is blocked so, at each bend in a river, the water pushes fastest around the outside of the bend and is slowest at the inside. Any constriction to a channel will speed up the flow. Obstacles in the current cause eddies or backwaters immediately downstream: here the water flows counter to the main current.

Tongues or chutes

Drifting down a rapid river with the current, the main flow of water between obstacles ahead will be indicated by inverted V-shapes in the current, the wider mouth of the V trailing off towards a point in the distance. Obstacles such as rocks, even just submerged, cause V-shaped trails in the

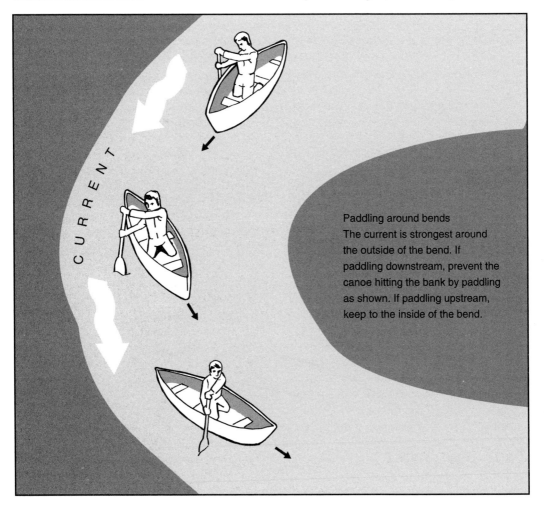

CURRENT

Paddling around bends
The current is strongest around the outside of the bend. If paddling downstream, prevent the canoe hitting the bank by paddling as shown. If paddling upstream, keep to the inside of the bend.

Eddies and a chute (tongue) caused by rocks.

water as the current runs past. The point of the V corresponds to the obstacle on the surface. If the obstacle is submerged, the point of the V will lie slightly downstream of the obstacle.

If you look at the water in a tongue or chute as it runs between two obstacles you will see that here, where the current is most restricted and flows fastest, the water is smooth. Further downstream, where the tongue narrows and the constriction has gone, the water is thrown into a series of waves. The tongue here is defined on either side by eddy lines, which are the turbulent borders between each eddy and the main current.

Eddy lines

The line of turbulence that divides the main current from the eddy is known as the eddy line. The eddy line is made up of little vortices and surges, most cleanly defined close behind the obstacle and more vaguely defined further downstream. The faster the water flow, the more turbulent this eddy line will become.

Paddling a river

When running a rapid river, watch constantly for

eddy lines. Aim your canoe down the centre of the chutes and avoid the points of the inverted V's because they indicate obstacles.

Follow the faster water around the outside of bends. Prevent your canoe being washed against the outside bank by aiming towards the inside of the bend. You will need to keep paddling forwards to keep your distance from the inside bank. Practice this technique of sliding round corners in safe situations where the bank on the outside of the bend is free of obstructions and no harm will come from a collision. This prepares you for more hazardous situations such as where the current runs through trees that might trap you.

Speed

You will only have steering control over the canoe if you travel faster or slower than the water. Otherwise you may point your canoe wherever you wish but the water will still carry you down the same path.

Travelling faster than the water is the usual way of making progress and, if the way ahead is straightforward and you can identify your route easily, then paddle forwards. However, as soon as you become uncertain about your route or need

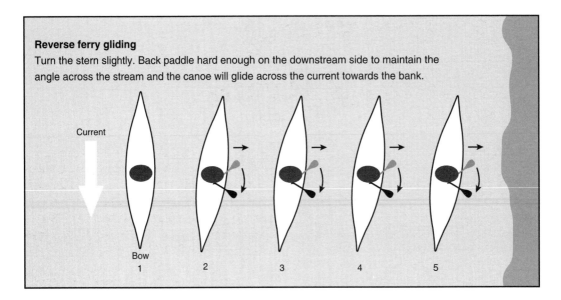

Reverse ferry gliding

Turn the stern slightly. Back paddle hard enough on the downstream side to maintain the angle across the stream and the canoe will glide across the current towards the bank.

Current

Bow

1   2   3   4   5

more time to make decisions, reverse. Now the direction in which your stern is pointing is the direction that you will move across the current. For example, if you wish to move across to the left side of the river you will need to point your bow to the right when reversing.

Ferry gliding

Ferry gliding is moving across a current without being swept downstream. You can do this facing upstream or down but, for river running, the downstream-facing or reverse ferry glide is probably the most important. It enables you to stop, review a situation or inspect the route ahead. In the event of a decision to land, to inspect, to portage or to wait, it enables you to cross safely to either bank.

First practice reversing against the current, maintaining your position relative to the shore. When you can comfortably keep your canoe in one position, turn the stern slightly to the in-side. The extra water pressure on the upsteam side of the canoe will start to turn it broadside. Paddle hard enough on the downstream side to counter the strength of the current and to maintain the

angle across the stream, and the canoe will glide across the current towards the bank. Re-align your canoe with the current, and hold your position. Now switch, and allow the stern to swing out in the other direction. Guide the canoe towards the opposite bank, reversing once more with the paddle on the downstream side.

As soon as you have mastered the technique of reversing on the downstream side to control your position, try controlling with the paddle on the upstream side. You will need to begin each stroke with a stern draw. The canoe will be easier to control if you let it swing out only a few degrees. If you let it swing out too far you will be swept broadside to the current and carried downstream.

Upstream-facing ferry glides are useful, particularly when paddling upstream from eddy to eddy. Turn the bow of the canoe so that it starts to swing out into the current, then paddle hard to maintain the angle, preventing the canoe from turning further as you cross the current.

One good way to move out into the current is to use a hanging draw or sideslip on the offside, (see chapter 13, Crossing Eddy Lines and chapter 7, Moving Sideways).

13 Crossing eddy lines

Eddies

Eddies are areas of water circulating in the opposite direction to the main current. They are found behind surface obstacles in the current, such as boulders, islands, bridge pillars and bays in the bank. Eddies are also found downstream of obstacles beneath the surface when the current is sufficiently strong.

Eddy lines

The dividing line between the eddy and the main current is known as the eddy line (see chapter 12). Normally the eddy line is defined by a wavering line of small vortices extending from the edge of an obstacle. When the speed difference between the eddy and the current is very great it is sometimes called an eddy fence because it can prove to be a barrier to the paddler.

Use of eddies

Eddies can be used as convenient stopping places in which to rest out of the current. They are invaluable as places to wait for members to catch up others in a paddling group, to make a landing or for inspecting the next section of river before committing to it. They also provide a means of working upstream.

Breaking into a current

Start by facing upstream in a large eddy with a clearly defined eddy line. Paddle towards the eddy line at an angle of about forty five degrees into the current. As your bow crosses the eddy line, the current will catch it and carry it downstream, quickly turning the canoe. Lean the canoe into the turn as you would a bicycle. (See chapter 9 for 'edging'.)

Turning towards the in-side, use a low brace for support, or a bow draw for a more positive grip on the current.

Turning towards the out-side, use a cross bow draw.

Doubles technique

The bow paddler performs either a bow rudder or a cross bow rudder while the stern paddler continues to provide forward power until the entire canoe has left the eddy. Timing is important. Paddling too rapidly may bring the canoe completely into the current before it has made a full turn, leaving you broadside to the current. A slightly slower approach will permit the canoe to turn through a wider angle before the stern finally leaves the eddy. Too slow an approach and you will make a complete turn downstream, but find yourself sitting on top of the eddy line rather than in the current.

Spinning on an eddy line

Align your canoe along the eddy line, facing upstream. For an in-side turn, use a bow draw to swing your bow out into the current, followed by

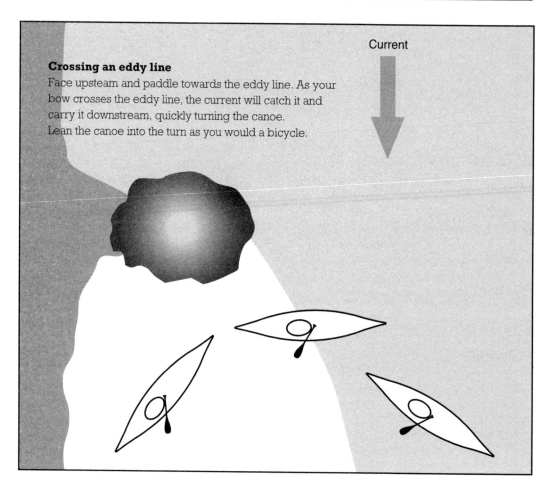

Crossing an eddy line
Face upsteam and paddle towards the eddy line. As your bow crosses the eddy line, the current will catch it and carry it downstream, quickly turning the canoe. Lean the canoe into the turn as you would a bicycle.

Current

a reverse stroke to push your stern back into the eddy. You should end up aligned with the eddy line once more, but facing in the opposite direction. For an out-side turn use a sweep stroke to push the bow out into the current. As the current swings the bow around, hook your stern in the eddy using a cross-stern draw. To spin once more, push the stern out into the current and the bow into the eddy. Your body should remain directly above the eddy line as you spin. Spinning on eddy lines is excellent practice for reading the movement of water and developing an awareness of how to make the water work for you rather than fighting against it.

Breaking out of the current

Paddle forwards across the current so that you cross the eddy line at speed. As you cross it, lean into your anticipated turn, which will be caused by the bow being held by the eddy while the stern is carried downstream by the current. A low brace or bow rudder will help your turn and add stability during an in-side turn, while a cross bow rudder will help you with an out-side turn.

Paddling tandem, the front paddler rudders while the rear paddler paddles forwards or braces for stability.

14 Lining, tracking and portaging

Lining is using lines from the security of the bank to control a canoe floating downstream. Tracking is controlling the canoe while pulling it upstream. Both techniques are used to negotiate shallow rapids where paddling may be difficult, or a loaded canoe too heavy to float. Lining and tracking can save the paddler wading with his canoe or portaging (carrying the canoe).

Attaching the lines

Two lines are generally used, one to the bow and the other to the stern, although a single long loop of line will serve just as well. The line to the upstream end of the canoe should be attached in such a way that it raises this end. A quick method of attachment is to tie a loop into the end of the line and pass it over the end of the canoe so that the knot lies underneath the bow. Thread a paddle beneath one thwart, over the loop of rope and beneath another thwart to hold the line

in position. The line at the downstream end of the canoe may be tied at a higher point to an end-grab or carrying handle. In this way the canoe, when held in the current, will float higher at the upstream end. Each line should be at least 15 yards (15 metres) long. More rope is needed for wider rivers although it is often easier to join on extra lengths of rope when required rather than cope with unwieldy lengths when less is needed. The rope should be sufficiently thick not to cut uncomfortably into your hands. Six millimetre diameter is a reasonable minimum, although thicker is more pleasant to handle. Out of preference I use braided floating line.

Tracking upstream

In order to tow the canoe offshore you will need to expose the inshore side of the canoe to the current. Prevent the canoe from drifting downstream by maintaining tension on the

Tracking upstream

Portaging

downstream line and feed out a little more line
to the upstream end to angle the canoe out from
the shore. As you walk up the bank, lead the
canoe behind you, keeping control by adjusting
one or both of the lines. Playing the canoe in the
stream is similar to flying a kite. All the time you
keep it at a reasonable angle to the current, the
canoe will 'lift' from the shore. Catch the current
on the wrong side of the canoe and it will 'drop'
straight back to your bank.

Lining downstream

The principles of lining are the same as for
tracking. Adjust the two lines so that the canoe
positions itself in the current where you want it .
With practice you should be able to guide your
canoe between rocks or around rocks as long
as there is sufficient clearance for your lines to
pass over the obstacles.

General comments

Lining and tracking are easier to manage from
the inside bank of a bend, or along a straight
section of river. Otherwise, if there is a degree
of choice, pick the bank that will make walking
easier.

Portaging

Portaging is the age-old technique of carrying
your canoe and gear overland from one stretch
of navigable water to another. When linking
between lakes on canoe routes or avoiding
waterfalls and other dangers, scout out the
easiest pathway for carrying before you commit
yourself. If you are going to use a carrying yoke
then you can easily follow a narrow trail but, for
carrying the canoe underhand, you will need a
broader path.

On routes where you expect to portage, try to
pack your gear in easily-carried bags. I've
carried unwieldy barrels along steep tracks
when, with forethought, I might have used a
rucksack. Rucksacks do not need to be
waterproof if the gear inside is stowed in
waterproof bags, but there are some very good
purpose-designed waterproof rucksacks
available.

Some well-used canoe routes are provided with
specially paved canoe portage paths. Here a
trolley is the easiest solution. Trolleys are easily
carried in open canoes, but beware: some
trolleys don't float!

15 Basic wave riding skills

In this chapter we'll look at riding standing waves - waves that stay in the same place.

The basic skills of wave riding are the ferry glide and the ability to control the canoe in a current without being swept downstream. The wave simply provides you with a ramp of water down which the canoe will run. The canoe runs downhill down the wave, stationary relative to the bank but speeding along relative to the water. In this position you only need to steer and trim the balance of the canoe to continue surfing the wave. Not all waves are suitable for surfing and some are dangerous so let's first look at some wave theory.

Standing waves

A constriction in a river will force the water to move faster, creating a gradient and a V-shape with the point of the V downstream. It also causes a wave or series of waves to form towards the point of the V, aligned to face the current. These waves remain in the same position relative to the bank, hence the name standing waves. As the water speeds up, these waves will steepen until the point of collapse is reached, when broken water will constantly tumble down the upstream face. Standing waves may appear as regular swells, breaking swells or as untidy heaps of water which burst sporadically.

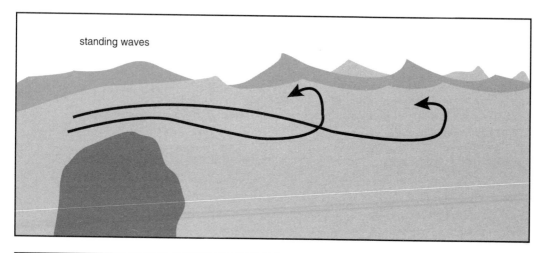

standing waves

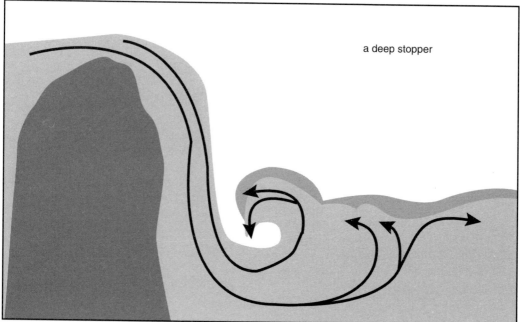

a deep stopper

Stopper waves (hydraulics)

Stoppers are vertical eddies with water
recirculating upstream at the surface. They are
called stoppers because they tend to stop
passing canoes or at least slow them down.
There are two main types of stopper: deep
stoppers and surface stoppers.

Deep stoppers

Deep stoppers form where water pours over a
slope or drop creating a strong downward
current. This downward current draws surface
water back upstream into the slot (the gap
between the descending water and the wave
crest). The surface current is called the tow-
back (sometimes backwash). A floating object

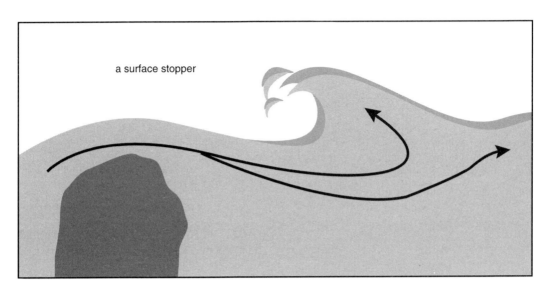

a surface stopper

in the slot may be forced down by the falling water, carried along by the current below the surface, to bob up again downstream of the fall. Then the surface tow-back takes over and drags it back to the fall again for a repeat cycle. The disturbing aspect of the cycle is that there is often no reliable exit from the trap for a swimmer. Deep stoppers do kill.

Deep stoppers are often characterized by a narrow slot and little evidence of a wave. The slot is turbulent but the water downstream looks calm and shows suspended bubbles. Close scrutiny reveals that the surface water is flowing back towards the fall. Look for the point at which water is surfacing, some to recycle and some to flow downstream. This will give an indication of the power of the hydraulic.

The more regular the drop and the stopper formed beneath it, the harder it is to escape. Man-made weirs are typically regular structures forming dangerous stoppers. Natural river features are seldom as regular and often have natural wash-though points which will eventually flush out canoes and swimmers. Do not be deceived by size. Even tiny stoppers can be extremely fierce.

Surface stoppers

Surface stoppers form when the angle of drop is slight. They can be extremely powerful, but a swimmer will be carried through by the swift downriver current flowing just beneath the turbulent surface. A buoyant canoe on the other hand will remain on the surface, trapped by the rush of the recirculating surface water.

Choosing a wave to ride

Begin with regular standing waves. Pick a place where a constriction has caused a clean chute of water to enter a pool, creating standing waves in the centre and an eddy to either side. Begin in the eddy at one side, facing upstream. Ferry glide out into the current from close behind the obstruction, upstream of the first wave. Paddle quickly so that the current carries you only slowly backwards to the wave. When the stern of the canoe is lifted by the wave, throw your weight forwards and accelerate.

Keep your canoe aligned directly into the current. As soon as you feel the canoe surge forward on the wave, ease off your paddling and

let the wave do the work. Steer using the bow rudder and stern draw. To exit the wave, simply steer towards the eddy on one side, or turn off the wave and paddle across into the eddy.

Once you can surf confidently facing upstream, try to reverse onto the wave and surf backwards.

Sidesurfing

Choose a broken wave, preferably a gentle surface stopper. Look for possible routes out of the stopper, such as a V-shaped break somewhere along its length, or a downhill slope towards one end. When viewed from above looking downstream, a 'smiling' shape is a friendly shape, with escape from the ends possible by moving downstream. A 'frowning' shape indicates that, in order to escape from the ends of the stopper, you will need to climb out against the current. Choose a stopper that angles away downstream.

Enter the stopper by surfing across it, then turn towards your paddle side using a stern rudder then a low brace. Lean your canoe downstream to present the bottom of the hull to the oncoming water, but try to keep the downstream gunwale just clear of the tumbling water from the wave. By using a bow draw you can lift the bow slightly higher up the wave than the stern, causing the canoe to slide backwards along the stopper or, by applying a stern draw, you can raise the stern

Stopper safety.

beware

OK

causing the canoe to slide forwards along the stopper.

When you wish to exit, move along to one end of the stopper as far as you can. If this is not sufficient to release you, slide rapidly forwards to the end of the stopper and reach forward abruptly with your paddle to grip the current running past the end of the stopper. You should now be able to draw the canoe out into the current. Make sure that the movement is fairly quick and that you do grab the current or you will find yourself reversing once more along the stopper.

Alternatively, begin a rapid reverse slide to the end of the stopper then reach back abruptly to grip the current passing behind you and draw the canoe backwards out of the stopper.

You can use the same basic technique to spin around in a stopper, switching sides. Surf to the end of the stopper and start to draw yourself out. When the canoe is aligned more or less straight into the current, the basic surfing position, steer it round into a sideways position facing the opposite direction. Now your paddle will be on the upstream side of the canoe. Either balance the canoe while you switch, or perform a cross-canoe low brace for balance and cross draws to bow and stern to steer.

16 Open water considerations

A Solvay Dory sailing canoe

Basic sailing

Sailing is a great way to extend the skills and thrills of travelling by canoe. A simple triangular sail called a 'lateen' is probably the simplest rig to use. You will need a short mast which is stepped to the stern thwart (the canoe is sailed backwards) and an additional spar, the gaff, which runs along the leading edge of the sail, effectively increasing the height of the mast. A third spar, the boom, runs along the lower edge of the sail.

Three lengths of line are used to rig and control this sail. The one used to raise the sail, the halyard, runs through a point near the top of the mast and attaches to the centre of the gaff. The lower end of the halyard should be held in position by a quick release cleat somewhere accessible near the centre of the canoe enabling you to lower the sail quickly if necessary.

The second line stops the boom from lifting. This is known as the boom vang. The vang is attached at one end to the boom and the other

end is led through a block at the mast foot to a cleat near the centre of the canoe.

The third line is used to control the angle of the sail to the wind. This line is known as the sheet. It attaches to the outer end of the boom and leads via a block to your hand. This gives you full control of sail adjustments and also enables you to free the sail from the wind quickly when needed.

When the canoe is sailing across the wind, it will slide sideways across the water unless there is something to provide resistance. In sailing dinghies and sailboards a centreboard or daggerboard provides this resistance. If you wish to customize a GRP (glass-reinforced plastic) or wooden canoe by fitting a centreboard slot, then this is an option open to you, but it is probably not worth doing unless sailing is to become your main means of propulsion. A less drastic modification is to fit one or two leeboards. These can be attached to a moveable thwart which clamps to the gunwale. There are two basic styles, one in which a single leeboard is dropped into a slot on whichever is the downwind side of the canoe. (The leeboard gunwale would be fitted with a suitable casing at each end.) The other style is to fit two leeboards, one at each side of the canoe, each able to pivot up to lie alongside the canoe. When sailing, the downwind board is swung down into the water and the upwind board is swung up out of the way to reduce drag. The downwind side of the canoe is the lee side of the boat, hence the name leeboard for the board that is dropped on the downwind side.

The final piece of rigging is the rudder. A

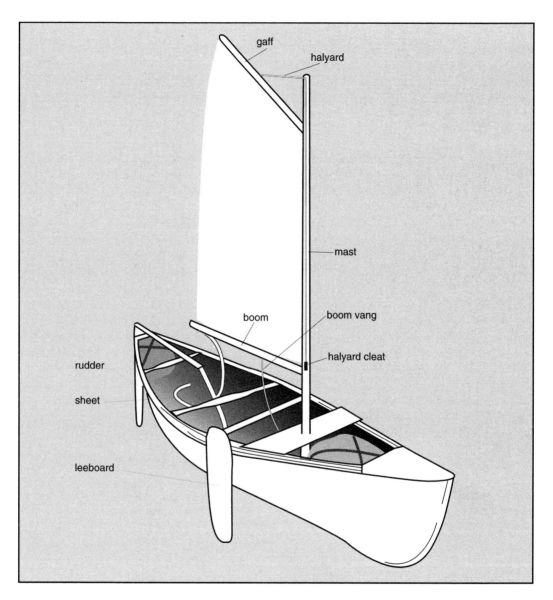

rudder is not strictly necessary, as it is perfectly acceptable to steer using your paddle, but it does make life easier. Most canoe rudders have a stock which matches the curve of the stern and is hung from the stern. The stock does not extend below the keel line of the canoe. From the stock the rudder blade pivots down below the keel line and can be swung out of harms way in shallow water. The rudder is normally controlled either by a tiller or by foot pedals.

Preparing the canoe for sailing

Your mast should be stepped somewhere between a quarter and a third of the way back from the end you will use as the bow. Estimate the position of the centre of effort of the sail by drawing a line from each corner of the sail to the mid point of the edge opposite. Where these lines cross is the centre of effort. Align the sail behind the mast along the centreline of the canoe. Now move the leeboard thwart until the leeboard in its dropped position is immediately below the centre of effort of the sail when viewed from the side of the canoe. This is roughly the position for the leeboard. You can fine tune this later when you have discovered how the canoe handles.

Step the mast in its upright position with the halyard threaded, and lay the sail with its gaff and boom along the thwarts inside the canoe. Raise the leeboards and rudder blade. Paddle the canoe away from the shore and point it into the wind.

Sailing

Lower both leeboards (one if you have only one). Use the halyard to raise the sail, then cleat it securely. Sit in the centre of the canoe and take hold of the sheet, checking that it is free of tangles. Use the paddle to turn the canoe across the wind and pull in on the sheet until the sail begins to fill. The canoe will start sailing forwards. It should also turn up into the wind again. To prevent this, steer with your paddle on the lee (downwind) side near the stern. If it is difficult to hold the canoe on a straight course across the wind because it is trying to turn upwind too strongly, then you may need to

This open canoe sailing group are enjoying a day on Lake Windermere.

move the leeboards a little further back. But it is desirable for the canoe to turn gently into the wind when the paddle is lifted out of the water. If the canoe turns downwind then the leeboards need to be moved forward until the canoe does turn upwind.

Now for sailing. Use your paddle to turn the canoe across the wind, then pull in on the sheet until the sail fills with air and you start moving forwards. Use your paddle on the lee side of the canoe near the stern to steer. Pulling in too much on the sheet will cause the canoe to heel over so, when steering a straight course across the wind, let out the sail until it just begins to flap, then pull in a little until it just stops flapping.

To turn the canoe around, lift your paddle from the water. The canoe should head up into the wind. Keep it turning by sweeping with your paddle until it lies across the wind once more. Trim your sail again by pulling in on the sheet until the sail just stops flapping. As the canoe begins to move forwards, steer with your paddle near the stern on the new lee side.

Water pressure will hold the paddle against the hull of the canoe on the lee side. This makes it possible to control the paddle with one hand, freeing the other to control the sheet.

When the wind becomes stronger, pressure on the sail will be enough to make the canoe heel over. To keep it upright either let the sail out a little, or move to the upwind side of the canoe and trim the canoe with your body weight. Shifts in your body weight can also help you steer. If you want to turn more quickly into the wind, move forwards and/or towards the lee side of your canoe when you take out your paddle. When you want to steer downwind, move back in the canoe to lighten the bow. You are using the same trimming weight shifts that you use when paddling the canoe.

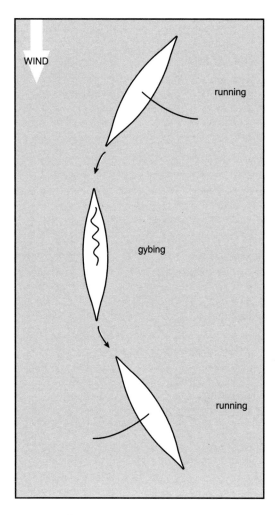

Running

Running is the term used to describe sailing downwind. The sail is let out until it lies at about right angles to the canoe. Move your weight back to lighten the bow. Be aware of where the wind is coming from at all times. If you change direction so that the wind catches the other side of your sail it can whip it violently across the canoe. To keep a margin of safety, run with the wind coming across the stern slightly, from the opposite side to the sail. Your leeboard is superfluous when you run downwind because there is no sideways push to resist, so pull it up to reduce drag.

To turn back across the wind from running, lower the leeboard, lean the canoe towards the lee side and pull in on the sheet. Steer with your paddle to prevent the canoe turning too far.

Gybing

Gybing is turning downwind until the wind catches the other side of the sail and pushes it across the canoe. To sail downwind the sail is let out until it extends out at about right angles to the canoe. When the wind is directly behind the canoe, the sail acts like a bag being pushed along by the wind. When you sail across the wind the sail behaves as a wing.

It makes no difference whether the sail is extended to one side or the other, you will move along just as effectively. To bring the sail across from one side to the other, first check that your leeboard is raised. Pull in a little on the sheet and steer slowly round towards the side on which the sail is lying. The fabric of the sail will slacken slightly just before the wind catches the other side of it. Watch for this warning that the sail is about snatch across the canoe and make sure that your head is not in the boom's path! Once the sail has crossed the canoe, switch sides with your paddle to the new lee side. You may turn across the wind in your new direction if you wish, but you will need to drop your leeboard once more.

Sailing upwind

It is possible to sail downwind with the sail filling like a bag or across the wind with the sail behaving as a wing but, if you steer directly into the wind, the sail collapses and the fabric simply flaps. This happens when you reach an angle of approximately forty five degrees from the wind. When you turn your bow through the wind (called tacking) you must continue to turn until the canoe is at least forty-five degrees from the

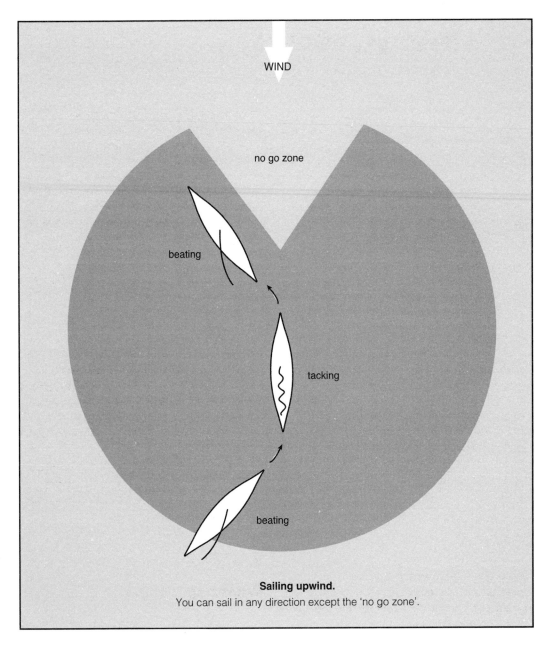

Sailing upwind.
You can sail in any direction except the 'no go zone'.

wind on the new side before the sail will function. So to make progress directly into the wind it is necessary to zig-zag. Sailing this zig-zag path is known as beating. The sail needs to be pulled in quite tightly to prevent it from flapping. Loss of wind from the sail usually indicates that you have turned too far into the

wind and need to steer away a little. If the canoe begins to heel over, you should be able to point a little higher into the wind. Often if the wind increases in strength you are able to point higher than in light winds. With any sailing into the wind (called close to the wind), your leeboard will need to be fully down.

The Beaufort Wind Scale

Force	mph	called	description
1	1-3	light	Direction of wind shown by drifting smoke.
2	4-7	light	Wind felt on face. Leaves rustle.
3	8-12	gentle	Leaves and small twigs in motion.
4	13-18	moderate	Small branches move.
5	19-24	fresh	Small crested waves form on inland waters.

Above force 5: unsuitable for canoe sailing.

Capsize

Capsizing a canoe with a sail is something you should practice in controlled conditions close to shore so that you are familiar with self rescue techniques before you need to use them for real. Sail across the wind, pull the sail in and lean your weight away from the wind.

Once in the water, keep hold of the canoe at all times. Remove the gaff from the mast, right the canoe, stow the sail with its gaff and boom, climb aboard and paddle the waterlogged canoe back to shore. Leave the leeboards down for stability.

Kites

Sailing with a kite is an excellent way to travel, especially for a tandem team, when the bow paddler can operate the kite while the stern paddler steers. Kites are used mostly for downwind sailing but, given adequate leeboards or with the equivalent use of paddles for the same purpose, it is possible to head up closer into the wind than is possible with a conventional sail. Do not attach your kite lines to the canoe while you steer. Should you fall overboard the canoe would sail away perfectly well without you. Always hold the control lines

yourself so that you can release them instantly should the need arise and carry a sharp knife in case you need to release tangled lines in a hurry.

Choose an easily operated kite that is steady in the air and has few strings to tangle. To begin with a modest kite will spur you on to continue: a complex or tricky kite is more likely to lead to frustration and failure. Discuss your requirements with a reputable kite dealer.

A wet kite is harder to launch into the air than a dry one. Practice launching and landing your kite on dry land before you try it from the canoe, and try wetting it.

SAFETY

Weather

Always obtain a weather forecast before deciding whether or not to sail. Practice in light winds to begin with and only go out in stronger winds when you are completely in control of all the basic manoeuvres. To start with, a wind of four to ten knots (Beaufort force two to three) would be plenty. With these wind speeds there may be steep wavelets on open water but very few breaking crests. Beware of a forecast indicating freshening winds, and of the approach of a cold front as wind speeds can increase suddenly and wind direction can change. If the wind does increase unexpectedly, you would be better advised to stow your sail and paddle back rather than try to sail in winds that are likely to capsize you.

Clothing

You will be colder sailing the canoe than paddling it, so you will need to dress more warmly and for possible immersion. Consider wearing a lightweight white water helmet as protection from the boom and, as sailing is less active than paddling, you may need gloves.

Paddles

Always carry at least one spare paddle. You may prefer a longer paddle than normal for steering, so carry a shorter one as your spare in case you end up paddling back after a capsize or a drop in the wind.

Anchoring

The best type of anchor to go for is probably a small CQR, which resembles a hinged ploughshare on a handle. Attached to the anchor you will need about three feet (1 metre) of chain, which will help the anchor cling to the bottom, and a long length of strong line. As a general rule the length of line needs to be between three and five times the depth of the water in which you anchor. So, if you wish to anchor in ten feet (3 metres) of water, you will need between thirty and fifty feet (10 to 15 metres) of line.

Attach the line to the canoe as for lining, with a loop passed over the end of the canoe and held in place by a paddle secured beneath the thwarts. This positions the pulling point beneath the hull near to one end, making for stability and allowing the canoe to point into the wind or current whichever is strongest. In emergency the anchor can be released by slipping out the paddle and sliding the loop off the canoe. As a precaution, tie a float to the end of the line so that you can always find the anchor should you slip the line accidentally or in a hurry. Check that the float is adequate to support the line before you use it. When stowing the anchor prior to moving onto deeper water, make sure it is secured to the canoe in its bag or drum so that it cannot be lost overboard.

Drogues

Drogues are anchors that grip the water rather than the bottom. They can be very useful for slowing downwind drift if you wish to rest on open water and will hold the canoe end-on into the wind while you relax, eat or fish. A plastic bucket serves well providing the handle is secure. Polythene buckets are less brittle than some other plastics. They can be drilled around the rim and threaded with line to replace the handle. Use the same 'beneath the hull' attachment technique as for anchoring and lining, and a long length of line. Holes drilled through the bottom will help stabilize the drogue, but a trip line to the narrow end of the bucket is not necessary. To retrieve the drogue simply haul in on the line until you can reach it. There are some good kayak drogues available that are ideal for canoes.

Paddling in waves

On choppy open water, keep the ends of your canoe light and buoyant by keeping the weight central.

When paddling parallel to breaking waves you

may prefer to paddle on the side from which the waves are approaching. This will enable you to use a low brace on the oncoming wave for balance, edging the canoe into the wave. Should the wave break, the hull of the canoe will then plane sideways across the water whereas an upright canoe tends to trip over itself.

Surfing a wave on open water requires a similar technique to surfing a river wave but the wave will change shape, developing from a swell into a steepening crest which will finally break towards the shore. When riding the wave shoreward, trim the canoe by moving your weight forward to aid acceleration down the wave, and by leaning or moving back to prevent the bow from burying as the wave steepens.

Your canoe must be well served with flotation bags or alternatives as you will almost certainly be swamped by any sizeable wave.

A spraydeck may be useful if you intend frequenting this kind of water. Spraydecks usually fasten either by small hooks, lacing or press studs around the gunwale. Wooden canoes sometimes have a keyhole-shaped groove around the gunwale to hold the spraydeck. They normally cover the canoe leaving holes where the seats are positioned for the paddlers. Some have built-in cockpit rims so that you can seal yourself in with an elasticated spraydeck as you would in a kayak. Generally, though, open canoeists use airbags in preference to decking their craft.

Clothing for open water

Dress for the water temperature. Should you capsize offshore it may be a little while before you are in a position to put on warmer clothing or find shelter from the wind. Once you are wet the wind will chill you more rapidly than when you are dry and you can chill even in seemingly warm weather. If you are not wearing windproofs, at least carry them in an accessible place ready to put on if the need arises.

For open water bailers and/or pumps are essential.

17 Poling

The standing position.

Poling is the fastest way of propelling a canoe upstream under human power. It can even be used for powering up rapids that cannot be ascended by paddling. It is an excellent tool for exploring small tributaries and creeks that would be tedious or impossible to negotiate using a paddle. Although the real forte of the pole is for upstream work, it can be useful for slowing your descent through rapids and to enable you to propel the canoe standing up, which on many rivers improves the view!

Poles

Canoe poles are normally between twelve and fifteen feet (four to five metres) long and are made of wood, glass reinforced plastic (GRP), or aluminium.

I like the feel of wood, but it is difficult to joint, so must be carried in one piece. To avoid splinters wood should be varnished and lightly rubbed down with wire wool to provide a comfortable surface to handle without becoming too slick when wet. Wood can also be bound with tape. Choose a diameter that is easy and pleasant to handle: something similar to the diameter of your paddle shaft, or slightly thicker, is fine.

The ends need protecting by some form of shoe or cap. Traditionally different types of shoe are used for different types of river bed. On a lake bed of soft mud the foot might have hinged flaps that fan out when pushed against the bottom, but hinge together to minimize resistance when the pole is raised through the water. For rocky rivers the protective sleeve and cap should end in a spike, reducing drag through the water but giving a good grip for jabbing on rock or gravel.

My own favourite is a take-apart GRP pole. I like it because it stows away easily in the canoe without intruding into my space. It is warm to the hands in winter and light in weight. It has a comfortable degree of flex so does not jar your hands.

Aluminium is the most popular material and is usually the cheapest option. A good grade will be flexible and light with a comfortable diameter. With the ends plugged, the pole will float and it is tough enough to withstand abuse. But bind the pole with tape to prevent your hands turning black.

The standing position

Stand about two thirds of the way down the canoe towards the stern so that the bow is light. Spread your feet about shoulder width apart, on the centreline of the canoe, facing the in-side. Swivel your front foot so that it lines up along the centreline of the canoe. It does help if you brace your front leg against a thwart.

The handover stroke

Drop the end of the pole onto the bottom just behind you. Climb hand over hand along the pole to push the canoe forwards, quickly sliding it back through your hands for the next push. You can push on the pole from a position just behind you. Once you are moving forwards this will mean dropping it in a little further ahead so that it is in position just behind you when it touches the bottom. Your hand grip will be the same as with a paddle for your bottom hand; hold the top hand so that you can view the inside of the wrist.

Windmilling

Windmilling

Make a short push without climbing your hands up the pole. Lift the pole out of the water behind you. Concentrating on the front end of the pole now, let go with your top hand for a moment while you drop the pole to the bottom again. Reposition your top hand, then readjust the grip with your bottom hand ready for your next push.

Steering

Steering is normally done as part of the forward poling stroke. To turn towards the in-side, push away sideways with your bottom hand and pull with your top hand. To turn towards the out-side, pull in on your bottom hand and push away with your top hand. All the effort is transmitted through your feet to the canoe, so help the process by exerting a twisting action on the canoe through your feet while you steer. Poling is a whole-body exercise.

Poling upstream

Windmilling and handover strokes work fine in gentle streams but, when the current gets faster, it is more effective to use short jabbing strokes, only lifting the pole a few inches (centimetres) from the bottom and only pushing the canoe along a few feet (about a metre) at a time. Keep the upstream end of the canoe light to aid control.

When poling upstream, look for eddies that you can use to help you and avoid the fastest part of the current whenever possible.

Poling downstream and snubbing

If you wish to travel faster than the water, pole normally, keeping the bow light. However, when the stream gets faster and when you are poling through rapids, you may wish to travel slower than the water. The technique you use then is called snubbing. Stand forward of the centre so that the bow is heavy, or you can simply turn the canoe so that you travel backwards, poling from your normal position. When the bow drifts to the right, snub or push with the pole at a point downstream on the right to bring the bow back again. If the bow drifts to the left, snub on the left. Use your feet to aid steering.

If you find that the current takes hold of the canoe and you are moving too fast to chance snubbing, trail the pole behind you and press it down onto the bottom to act as a brake.

Other techniques

Poling opens up a whole range of techniques. Try using the pole like a kayak paddle. Although there is no blade there is a surprising amount of purchase on the water and certainly enough to push you along at speed. Hold the pole in the centre and slide both hands out equally until they are about shoulder width apart. Stand in your normal poling position, keeping the bow of the canoe light. Keep your arms extended in front of you, so that you can make full use of torso rotation, and paddle on alternate sides.

Try paddling with the pole in deep water just on one side of the canoe.

Try some of the other canoe paddle techniques using a pole instead of the paddle. For example, try the bow rudder and the draw stroke.

18 Alternative forward paddling techniques

Paddling options

There are a number of variations on the forward stroke, all linked to different steering methods and suitable for different conditions. They are all for straight-shafted paddles rather than bent shafted paddles, for which switching is the only useful option.

Goon stroke

The goon stroke is similar to a J stroke except that the steering phase uses a push-away with the back of the blade instead of the power face. It probably causes more drag in the water than a J stroke, so is less efficient. However, the extra stability it offers makes it a valuable option for the white water paddler and for those attempting to master balance in a tippy canoe.

Pitch stroke

This is a smooth action with the steering phase integrated by changing the angle of the blade during the power phase of the stroke. Start with

The pitch stroke. Start with your blade angled for maximum grip on the water. Halfway through the power phase, start rotating your blade, power-face out. By the end of the power phase your blade should be angled out at about forty five degrees. Clip the blade propeller-style from the water behind you.

your blade angled for maximum grip on the water as usual. When you have completed about half of the power phase, start rotating your blade, power face out. By the end of the power phase your blade should be angled out at about forty five degrees. Clip the blade propeller style from the water behind you.

C stroke

The C stroke is the name given to a forward stroke where a bow draw is added at the start of a J stroke. It is particularly useful when starting from standstill and in some conditions of wind or current.

Knifed J (Canadian stroke)

The knifed J begins as a J stroke but, in the steering phase, the blade is rotated only sufficiently far to drop the outer edge of the blade slightly lower then the edge nearest the canoe. The blade is then skimmed forwards under the surface rather than above. The blade remains angled in such a way that it will try to dive. Resist this tendency by pulling up on the paddle as you guide it out from the side and forward. It is this resistance that provides the steering effect. The knifed J is a relaxing stroke for touring.

Indian stroke

The knifed J (Canadian stroke). Skimming the blade forward under the surface provides the necessary steering method.

The Indian stroke is a very quiet way of moving forward. The paddle blade remains in the water throughout. The stroke begins as a bow draw (see chapter 7), and continues as a J stroke. At the end of the J, rotate your top hand on the grip and slice the paddle forwards into a position for a bow draw. What was the back of the blade now becomes the power face for the next stroke which continues without pause. By varying the amount of bow draw and the degree of correction used with the J, and by angling the blade slightly when you edge it forwards, steering can easily be incorporated.

Because the blade never leaves the water, the visible movement of the paddler is less than with other paddle strokes. This, together with the lack of splash, makes the Indian stroke particularly good for approaching wildlife.

The Indian stroke is a quiet way of moving forward. Note that the paddle remains in the water throughout.

19   A day trip

Be self-sufficient

A well prepared canoeist should carry sufficient
equipment to cope with any likely emergency. It
is better to be self-sufficient than rely on outside
help. Let's look at some situations that do occur
and how you might deal with them.

- You damage your canoe, causing it to leak.

Temporary repairs can usually be made to
allow completion of your planned trip. Use duct
tape or cloth-backed adhesive waterproof tape
to cover small holes or cracks. If the hole is too
large to be repaired in this way, use the same
tape to secure a patch of stiff polythene over the
hole. These types of tape only stick when the

hull has been thoroughly dried. Rub the
surrounding area with a dry cloth. If necessary
you can complete the drying process by
pouring a drop of alcohol (methylated spirit or
ethanol) onto the area and igniting it. This warms
and dries the repair site. Be careful to avoid
accidental spillage which might ignite
surrounding vegetation or indeed your canoe!
Use only a drop to begin with until you are
familiar with the effect.

Plumbers' mastic tape is a grease-impregnated
tape that will stick to a wet surface. It is useful for
on-the-water repairs and for rainy weather
repairs, but the grease does transfer easily to
clothing and skin, and the patch will scrape off
easily if you rub against a rock.

> **Basic repair kit.**
>
> Broad adhesive waterproof tape.
> Sheets of stiff polythene as patches.
> Plumbers' mastic tape.
> Methylated spirit for cleaning mastic from
> hands and for warming repair site.
> Matches/lighter.
> Disposable plastic gloves.
> Dry rags.
> Scissors and/or knife.

> **Basic first aid kit**
>
> A triangular bandage.
> Melanin gauze dressing (for burns).
> Crepe bandage.
> Plasters.
> Adhesive tape.
> Headache tablets.
> Petroleum jelly (to prevent excessive
> drying of skin).
> Sterile strips/sutures for open wounds.
> Disposable protective gloves.
> Scissors.
> Tweezers.
> A small pair of pliers (for emergencies
> such as cutting and extracting fish hooks).
> Eye bath.
> Pencil and paper.
> Snake bite kit.
> Insect repellent.
> Antihistamine in case of bite allergy.
> First Aid Afloat (a Fernhurst book)

- Someone requires first aid.

Always carry a basic first aid kit. Likely emergencies and solutions include:
a sore thumb – plasters and a reel of adhesive tape
a snake bite – snake bite kit
sunburn – calamine lotion
a splinter – tweezers.

Tailor your first aid kit to your needs: if your country has no biting snakes then a snake bite kit is superfluous. When you paddle with other people it is also useful to be aware of any medical conditions or allergies suffered by your companions.

- Someone shows signs of the onset of hypothermia.

Hypothermia is a dangerous fall in body temperature, which can lead to unconsciousness and death if not treated. In canoeing the common causes of hypothermia are cold water immersion and exposure to the wind when wet. Provided it is fit and well, the body can usually maintain its normal temperature if fuelled with food and insulated by adequate clothing to prevent excessive heat loss. Clothing that appears suitable may not be adequate to cope with immersion in cold water.

Shivering is the body's first natural response to cold. This involuntary movement of the muscles provides heat but uses the body's fuel reserves. If shivering starts, put on more clothing, eat and have a hot drink. If shivering continues, then it is time to find shelter or finish your paddling session. If you notice someone else shivering, follow the same procedure.

Hypothermia follows when the body has insufficient reserves to maintain normal body temperature. First the blood supply to the extremities is reduced, which cuts down heat loss and gives the skin a white or bluish tinge. Shivering stops. The brain and other vital body organs are kept at a working temperature at the expense of less essential functions. The ability to think clearly or make a reasonable judgment is lost, speech often becomes slurred, and the ability to keep balance is commonly lost. Collapse is soon followed by unconsciousness

Basic cold emergency kit.

Exposure bag or survival shelter.
Spare clothes, to include water/windproof
layer and warm dry layer, including hat
and gloves in cold weather or when
paddling on cold water.
Hot drink (a vacuum flask is the best way
of providing a hot drink instantly, but a
stove, matches/lighter, pan and fresh
water, with choice of drink flavourings
makes a good back-up).
Emergency food.

Basic emergency/distress equipment

VHF radio (you may need a licence).
Distress flares.
Bright orange flag (your exposure bag
would do if it is orange).
Whistle.

Additional items that could prove
invaluable are:

Map
Compass
Waterproof watch
Radio (for listening to weather forecasts)
Basic tool kit (knife, pliers, screwdriver)
Bailers
Anchor with chain and line
Torch with batteries.

and death unless treated immediately, so any
one of the early symptoms should be viewed
with suspicion and protective action taken
before things get out of hand.

The immediate priority should be the removal of
the person from the source of cold (out of water,
out of wind). Then insulate with extra protective
clothing or within an exposure bag or shelter
tent etc. Provide food and a warm drink as
additional sources of energy. Encourage quiet
rest and seek medical assistance.

A shelter from the wind can be made by turning
the canoe on its side, hull against the wind, using
the paddle as a prop. (See chapter 20 on
camping.)

Prevention is better than cure. Be aware of how
fit you are, including whether or not you have
slept well, eaten well or are recovering from a
cold. Be aware of your anxiety level and your
level of all-round fitness: both can affect your
susceptibility to hypothermia. Dress according
to conditions and put on more clothing if you feel
cold. Eat snacks or take warm drinks if you feel
hungry between meal stops.

- Someone is unable to continue to shore.

You can tow another canoe. Consider taking the
incapacitated paddler aboard your own craft as
a passenger before rigging a towing harness
around the bow of his craft and using your stern
painter as a towing line. You will need a length
of rope or stern painter at least fifteen feet (five
metres) long.

- Someone breaks or loses a paddle.
  Always carry a spare paddle, otherwise you
  could find yourself carrying a passenger and
  towing his canoe.

- You cannot deal with an emergency on your
  own and need to call for outside help.

Attract attention visually using a bright orange
flag, waving a paddle in the air, firing a distress
flare, or use sound by blowing on a whistle or
calling on VHF radio. Your options may be
limited in the area in which you are paddling.

The international distress signal on a whistle is

three short blasts followed by three long blasts, followed by three more short blasts (Morse code for SOS).

Carrying your safety equipment.

Most paddlers use waterproof 'dry-bags' or a plastic barrel or drum. Gear may also be stored in watertight end lockers if your canoe is fitted with them (they are often available as optional extras).

Securing bags in your canoe
There are several different schools of thought.

- Tether your bags with lines long enough for you to lift the bags out of the canoe when you need to empty out water. Rescue on water can be awkward with the lines tangling, but the lines will permit some degree of shifting of the load to trim the canoe in changing conditions.

- Tie your bags securely so they cannot budge. This makes managing the canoe in the water easier following a capsize, but

draining it a little more difficult. Trimming your canoe by moving gear becomes harder.

- Leave your bags loose so they float out during a capsize. You will have an uncluttered canoe during the rescue but will have to round up the bags afterwards. It is essential that they float. Moving weight around to adjust trim is straightforward. On moving water, some maintain that it is easier to recover a swamped canoe without the added burden of cargo, which can be rounded up later further downstream.

Securing small items

Judging by the volume of small items retrieved by snorkeling beneath small falls, it is well worth securing small items such as sunglasses, hats, bailers, money wallets, car keys, cameras and binoculars to prevent their loss in a capsize. Some items can be attached to your person and others to the canoe. Remember that, unless you can zip your pockets closed, keys and cash will drop out during a capsize and swim.

Some basic safety considerations

- Group size. Too large a group will become difficult to monitor and spreads easily. If you have a large group, consider dividing it into smaller groups, each self-sufficient, and arrange for regular meeting places along the route. For rescues, at least two canoes are needed.

Three is a good minimum number. If one canoe meets with an accident, there are two more, one to go for help and another to remain with the victim of the accident.

- Is your proposed trip suitable for all members of your party? Consider the distance, level of difficulty of the water and the weather forecast in relation to your direction of travel. Find out the experience level of the party in terms of paddling skills and rescue expertise.

- On open water, will you be paddling into or away from the wind? If both, then it is better to paddle against the wind to start with, so that you have its help later when you are not so fresh.

- Will there be dangers such as weirs, falls or strong currents to negotiate?

- Plan for alternative exit points from the river in case things do not go according to plan.

- Let somebody responsible know where you intend to paddle and what time you intend to return. Tell them what you would like them to do if you are unduly late. For example, call for help.

Environmental considerations

Many of the finest paddling areas are sensitive to disturbance or damage. Reed beds often shelter nesting birds. Easily damaged mosses, liverworts and ferns frequently carpet potential portage points. Loons and ospreys nest on lake islands. Fish spawn in gravel beds in rivers. Find out about the area where you plan to paddle. There may be places to avoid but, on the other hand, there may be wildlife to watch. Be considerate and don't spoil something special through ignorance or lack of awareness. During portages (carrying the canoe overland) don't drag the canoe through the undergrowth and don't leave litter. It does help if you collect and bring out pieces of litter you find on the way. Avoid contamination when urinating by retreating at least 150 feet (fifty metres) from the water. Try to leave no trace of your passing!

Keep together

By keeping together as a group you will be in a position to help one another and be aware of each other's needs. You will be safer as a group than as individuals on the water.

20 Camping

Choosing a site

When you are looking for a place to camp, consider the priorities listed below.

Is there easy landing?

Occasionally I pick a place to camp where the landing is awkward if the site promises to be especially good. However, I gain satisfaction from being able to step out of my canoe, lift one end ashore, unload and set up camp within a few feet (a metre or two) of the canoe. It is worth either tethering the canoe or lifting it completely ashore to avoid losing it if the water level rises or the wind increases.

Is there fresh water available?

You have several alternatives regarding drinking water on camping trips. You may be able to carry sufficient fresh water for your whole trip. If you are paddling an area where the water quality is good, you might be able to find a source of fresh water each night. There are chemical treatments you can use to 'purify' water or, in some areas, simply boiling the water for a few minutes will suffice. If you camp a lot consider investing in a water filter. Water will constitute a major part of your load if you need to carry enough for a whole trip.

Dispose of water used for washing or washing-up well away from the water source to avoid polluting it.

Is there natural shelter from the wind?

Shelter from the wind can be both an advantage and a disadvantage. It will protect your tent and cooking areas from a battering but the wind can keep most biting insects away. I seek shelter in windy weather, but exposure in quiet weather.

Is there sufficient flat ground for your tent or shelter?

Look for flat, well-drained ground. If there is any chance of rain, try to imagine where the water will drain and avoid those areas. The type of vegetation will often indicate which areas are prone to waterlogging.

Will you be inconspicuous?

Being hidden may protect you from unwelcome attention from passers-by and increase your chances of spotting wildlife. You will be hampered if you have a brightly-coloured canoe or tent.

Are you safe from rising water levels?

Some rivers and lakes can rise considerably as a result of rain elsewhere, while you are experiencing fine weather. Rivers tend to rise more rapidly in narrow gorges than on wide open stretches. Look for evidence of the water level having been higher. Sometimes twigs, grasses and other debris will be lodged in bushes and along the high water line of lakes and rivers, showing how high the water can get. Try to get a weather forecast for the upper reaches of your river/lake system and, if in any doubt, seek somewhere higher to camp.

Are you safe from lightning?

Some areas are noted for thunderstorms so, if there are electrical storms about, you must choose an area safe from lightning. If possible, camp on dry or well-drained ground, away from summits but not in cave entrances or under overhangs that might become spark gaps. Look for signs of trees that have been struck by lightning; signs such as scorch marks down the trunk, trees with bark peeling from the trunk or even the charred stump where a tree has been completely burned. Trees that have been struck once are obviously situated in places that could be struck again and are not good places to camp. Remember that the effect of a lightning strike will extend into quite a large area surrounding the point of impact. A site among low trees where there are more prominent trees at a little distance should be a safe position. Always leave the water when thunderstorms approach.

Are you likely to be troubled by wild animals?

Research unfamiliar areas for possible problems before venturing into them. Some animals cause minor irritation but others can be dangerous. I have had food packets opened and the contents scattered by mice but I am much more careful with food in areas where there are bears. Look around potential campsites for recent signs of animals, check sand and mud for prints and look for regular animal pathways. If the area shows evidence of being a busy highway, it might not be a good spot for you.

Will you disturb wildlife?

When you check for signs of wildlife, be aware of any nests or birds being disturbed by your presence. Camping too close to birds nests may well lead to the birds abandoning their eggs or young. Be sensitive and move to a less disruptive site.

Are insects likely to be troublesome?

Biting flies are the most common troublesome insects around water. There is little you can do to avoid them except camp where there is a little breeze and/or apply insect repellent. Ticks are common in some areas and usually cling to the tops of grasses and other tall plants and shrubs. Tuck your trousers into your socks to limit access to your skin and try to brush away ticks from your clothing before entering your tent. Examine your skin frequently and remove ticks by grasping firmly between finger and thumb nails and pulling as with a protruding splinter. Insect repellent will make your skin less attractive, even to ticks.

Some colours attract bugs more than others. Yellow seems a favourite whereas green seems to be left alone.

Tents/shelters

A wide variety of lightweight tents are readily available nowadays. However, many paddlers prefer to rig up their own lightweight shelters using either a tarpaulin or a sheet of lightweight canvas or nylon. One commonly used method is to prop your canoe on its side using one or two paddles as props. You may get sufficient shelter beneath the canoe angled like this, with the hull towards any wind, but a sheet of fabric pegged out from the side of the canoe using a canoe pole as a ridge will make a more extensive and weatherproof shelter.

For cooking among trees, suspend a tarp over a suitable patch of ground to keep off rain. Plenty of line is needed to tie it. In rainy conditions it is useful to rig an additional line across beneath the tarp to create a ridge. This will prevent water pooling in the centre. Rig the line in such a way that your chosen entrance is not one of the draining edges.

In Denmark there are a number of specially rigged canoes with hoop poles between the gunwales and tents that cover these hoops. The canoe becomes the waterproof groundsheet and tent walls. The canoe needs to be specially modified so that there are no thwarts intruding into your space and the seats can be moved for sleeping.

Cooking

Cooking on a camping stove has the least impact on your camping area. If you must have a fire, build it on sand or carefully remove an area of turf so that you will not damage the vegetation. Do not build fires on flat slabs of bedrock. Although they are safe areas, fires scar the rock more or less permanently and will always be obvious to future visitors. When you have finished with your fire, extinguish it completely, preferably dousing the area with water to cool it down, then replace any turf. Replacing turf onto a still-hot surface will dry out the turf, killing the vegetation and may also rekindle the fire.

However you are cooking, be careful not to spread fire.

Waste and rubbish

Carry out any waste or rubbish. It will help improve your paddling environment if you also carry out litter dropped by others. If you burn your rubbish, collect any remains when the fire has been extinguished and carry them out. It is a good idea to carry a special rigid container for rubbish to separate it from other gear and so that sharp edges cannot protrude.

21 Canoe and equipment design

There are many types of open canoe, each shaped to give particular handling characteristics. If cargo carrying is a major consideration then your canoe will probably be broad, stable and long, with little or no rocker and lot of freeboard. A V-shaped hull or a keel will help it track straight and give the hull more stiffness for carrying weight .

On the other hand if you intend to use your canoe only on sheltered water and you are seeking effortless cruising, then a long narrow canoe with little freeboard will serve you better. You will find it less stable but much easier to push through the water and there will be less above the water for the wind to catch. A little tumblehome (inward slope from the widest part of the canoe to the gunwale) often helps to keep water from slopping over the low sides and the bow and stern will be thin to slice through the water. Such a canoe would be impractical for rough water. The fine bow would plunge excessively and water would pour over the sides.

If you want to play on white water, then you will probably choose a more manoeuvrable canoe with a flattish bottom and a lot of rocker (curvature in the hull from bow to stern). A lot of freeboard, often combined with a degree of tumblehome, helps keep the water out. Forward speed becomes less important than manoeuvrability, so a white water canoe is typically short. This also makes it responsive to weight shifts, so it can be trimmed quickly by the paddler leaning forward or back. But, of course, it is not fast in a straight line and does not track well.

Bow and stern shapes are full and buoyant compared to the fine, low volume bow and stern of a flat water cruiser.

So what are the main factors of design? Well, build the canoe longer and narrower and it becomes faster, tippier and straighter running. Make it shorter and broader and it becomes slower, more stable and more manoeuvrable. Build the hull deeper and it will cope with waves without shipping water, but will catch the wind. With a shallower hull, the canoe will be less affected by the wind, but less able to cope with rough water without your getting wet.

The flatter the hull beneath you the more initial (bolt upright) stability you have. As the cross section of the hull gets closer to a semicircle, the less initial stability you have and the tippier the hull becomes.

Secondary stability

Secondary stability is the stability of the canoe when it is leaned. A semicircular cross-section to the hull gives almost no secondary stability. Once the canoe starts rolling, it will continue to roll. A flat-bottomed canoe with vertical sides will resist rolling as the chine (the angle between hull and side) is pushed down into the water. There will come a point when the canoe will suddenly flip. The same flat bottom with sides that flare out at an angle will resist rolling just the same initially but, when the canoe is ready to flip, the flared side comes to rest on the water, resisting capsize (secondary stability).

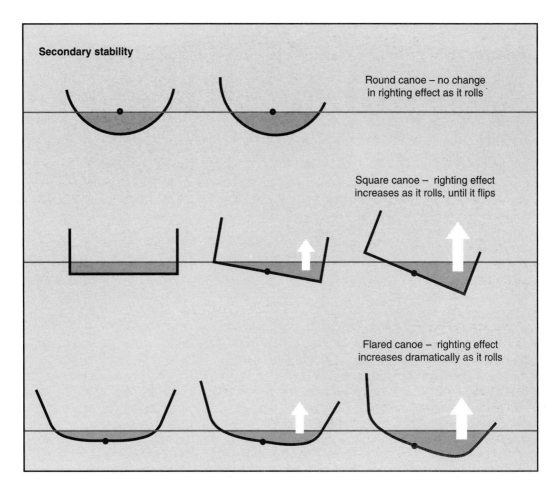

Secondary stability

Round canoe – no change in righting effect as it rolls

Square canoe – righting effect increases as it rolls, until it flips

Flared canoe – righting effect increases dramatically as it rolls

The disadvantage? You now have a canoe with a greater beam for the same initial stability.

If you want your design to be easier to lean, you can make the flat bottom narrower, curve the bottom or incorporate a shallow V-shape. The more gradual the transition between the bottom and the side, the less abruptly you will lose balance when leaning.

Some canoes have tumblehome. This can help keep water out of the canoe when it is leaned and it can leave you a little more clearance for your hands from the gunwale while paddling. However, it makes emptying the canoe on its side harder. Tumblehome is often used on white water canoes and on shallow flatwater canoes.

Then there is rocker. Surf wildly down a steep wave and a highly-rockered canoe will run straight on where a canoe with less rocker will have to turn or its bow will bury itself in water. But, to paddle along a lake, the canoe with a lot of rocker will need constant work to keep it on course while the less rockered canoe will track more easily. Rocker gives you manoeuvrability at the expense of straight tracking.

Canoe construction

Most touring craft are constructed from plastic, aluminium or glass-reinforced plastic (GRP).

Plastic canoes are moulded in one piece and

fitted afterwards with gunwales, thwarts and seats. The plastic is generally warm to touch, quiet on impact and probably tougher than equivalents in either GRP or aluminium. Plastic tends to bounce on low impact and dent on high impact. It slides on rock although the surface of some plastics will scuff readily and fur with abrasion. Dents can often be eased out by warming the area and pushing back into shape.

Aluminium may have a longer useful life than plastic or GRP - an advantage if you intend to paddle the same canoe for a lifetime. However, aluminium is noisy, dents on impact and tends to stick onto rock rather than sliding. It is also cold to touch and can leave black metallic marks on your clothing. Aluminium canoes come ready-fitted although there are various specifications to choose from, including different types of keel. If damaged, dents can be carefully beaten out and new plates can be riveted in position if the skin is broken.

GRP offers some of the cheapest options for canoes and the biggest variety of design in mass production. The material allows much sharper and more accurate shapes to be built. In production, a water-resistant gelcoat is followed into the female mould by layers of glass cloth or matting which are then saturated with resin. Unfortunately this leaves the rough worked surface on the inside which is not ideal for comfort. Each canoe is hand built, so it is possible to customize with myriad colours or graphics, and to vary the weight of lay-up. By incorporating different materials such as diolen, Kevlar and carbon fibre, it is possible to increase stiffness and/or cut down weight without sacrificing strength or making the skin less tear resistant. Many competition canoes are made in this fashion using combinations of materials to produce very lightweight rigid craft. In use, GRP canoes tend to slip better on glancing impact than plastic or aluminium, keeping their hard smooth outside finish, but shatter on higher impact.

Traditional materials are seen less often nowadays but wood-strip canoes are still built. Hand-crafted, using narrow planks secured over a wooden frame, these light durable canoes withstand impact well. Wood is a good insulator and it floats, but it does need to be protected by varnish or by sheathing in GRP. You pay the price for one of these works of art at purchase but, with love, care and maintenance, it could last you a lifetime.

An easy home-building option, which can produce lightweight canoes cheaply and quickly, is offered by the "kayel" construction method of stitched and glued plywood. Plywood panels are cut to a pattern, laced together with copper wire or nylon line and then joined using epoxy resin or GRP. The shell is then fitted out with thwarts and seats and painted or varnished before use.

Racing canoes are often built out of overlapping sheets of veneer. This method of construction produces a canoe that is rigid, lightweight and strong. Some recreational canoes are produced in the same way, using contrasting shades of veneer to beautiful effect. These are expensive and are likely to be looked after to the point of becoming family heirlooms!

Canoe storage and maintenance

A canoe is best stored under cover or stored upside down off the ground on racks. Wood will need checking regularly for damage. Signs of darkening of the wood in patches generally indicates the intrusion of water through damaged varnish. Strip the varnish from the darkened areas, dry out thoroughly, remove any softened wood and revarnish the affected area.

Aluminium canoes need checking to ensure that the rivets are intact. Loose rivets may cause leaking and, eventually, sections of aluminium will become loose and prone to catch on rocks causing further damage.

Thwarts and seats are generally fitted to plastic canoes with bolts. Ensure that the nuts are kept tight. Gunwales are frequently riveted. Check rivets for looseness and re-rivet if necessary using aluminium or stainless steel rivets.

Check over GRP canoes for signs of damage to the gelcoat layer on the outside. Any damaged outside areas should be checked inside too for damage to the laminations. Remove any loose gelcoat, cut out any shattered glass laminations and wet-and-dry to rough up the surface prior to repairs. Ensure that the canoe is clean and thoroughly dry before replacing gelcoat or repairing laminations.

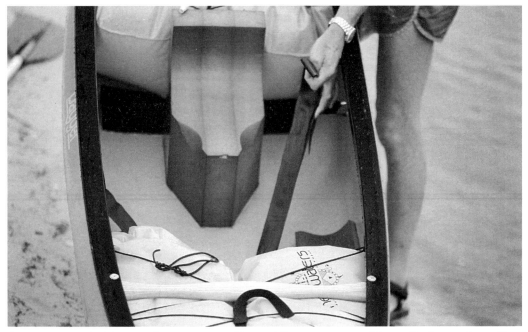

It is recommended that you fit your canoe with a saddle-seat or central foam plinth, together with thigh straps, knee pads and foot braces.

Seating

For general touring your seat may be constructed from a simple plank of wood, a piece of shaped plastic or a more comfortable cane seat. With wood it may be necessary to round a few edges and pad for comfort. Foam knee braces or pads are easily glued into position in the canoe using a strong contact cement. Lightly coat the foam with a thin, even film of cement. Allow to dry thoroughly before applying a second film to the foam and to the inside of the canoe where the foam is to be attached. Leave the coated surfaces open to the air until almost touch dry before pressing the foam firmly into place.

White water canoes are generally customized with a saddle seat or pedestal which either bolts in position or, in the case of a closed-cell foam pedestal, is glued into place. Such seats are normally complemented with knee supports or pads, thigh straps and foot braces. If you are the only person likely to use the boat, then a wedge of solid foam makes an ideal lightweight foot brace, otherwise adjustable kayak footbraces may be better. Thigh straps are anchored by means of rings glued into position between your knees and to each side. Straps should provide you with a firm grip on the canoe for control but you must be able to exit easily. Buckles or Velcro are the usual quick-release options but the straps should be positioned so that escape is possible without resorting to the quick-release system.

Thwarts

For white water paddling you will need more strengthening thwarts in your canoe than you will for gentle water. Figure out where the longest stretches of unbraced gunwale are and lie your extra thwarts there, across the canoe.

Now check to see whether they interfere with your range of seating positions or compromise your free exit. When you are happy with the positions, trim and fit to the gunwales. If your canoe has a carrying yoke, check that it is still at the point of balance. You may need to adjust its position but this final adjustment is best carried out after all other modifications have been completed. Factors to be considered include fitting a saddle seat, foot braces, buoyancy bags and any other items that may affect the balance point of the craft. Then unbolt the carrying yoke and find the new comfortable carrying position by resting it across your shoulders and gently sliding the canoe along until it balances.

Paddles

There is a bewildering variety of paddles available nowadays. They differ in the shape and size of the blade and in the materials from which they are constructed. There is also wide variation in the angle between the blade and shaft and the shape of the shaft. It may be useful to differentiate between the paddles used for different purposes.

Blade shape

For white water, where the depth may be small but the ability to accelerate and decelerate quickly is essential, a fairly short but broad blade is good. This shape has been widely adopted also for general purpose paddle sport, for use in rafts, sailing dinghies, and for powerboats in shallow water.

For general purpose touring on deep water, long narrow-bladed paddles perform well. They do not provide such good acceleration as broad, short blades, but are great for moving a laden boat along steadily using the range of paddle-and-steer strokes. Commonly recognized shapes such as the beavertail and

the ottertail resemble the shapes of the tails after which they are named. Ottertails are more vulnerable to damage in shallows than the broader-ended beavertails but, personally, I prefer the feel of the ottertail in the water.

Bent shaft paddles

Bent shaft paddles are good for touring and racing. They have only one bend, at the throat just above the blade. The angle of bend is normally between six and fifteen degrees. You will need to use a short stroke and change sides by switching instead of steering. By switching, all your energy goes into forward speed with no steering component and you use the muscles on both sides of your body equally. However, only one side of the blade is used as the power face, the side on the outside of the bend, so the paddle is not so versatile if you are doing a lot of manoeuvring. Paddlers generally use a smaller angle of bend when paddling solo than when paddling tandem. The plus is that the angle of the blade to the water is better for applying power than with a straight shaft.

Crank-shafted paddles

Crank-shafted paddles have a curved shaft to bring your hand more comfortably in line with your wrist when you are in the forward paddling position. Because the crank limits your alignment to using only one face of the blade as the power face, it is often found in combination with a bent shaft. The snake-like shaft may look odd but it feels very comfortable in use.

Hand grips

The shapes and sizes of hand grips vary. Look for the style you prefer and choose a grip that is comfortable and fits your hand. The T-shape, which a lot of white water paddlers favour, offers

Traditional paddles

Palm
grip

Beaver tail　　Otter tail

General purpose and white-water paddles

T-grip

tight control with the fingers wrapping around the bar of the T. The palm and scroll types offer a more relaxed grip.

The palm grip is generally symmetrical front and back, allowing either blade face to be used as the power face with the grip feeling the same each way round. This makes forward paddling styles such as the Indian stroke comfortable. Rotation is easier through the hand without the arms of a T.

The scroll grip is similar but is not symmetrical front to back. It is designed for one-sided use so one side is contoured to suit the fingers, the other to fit the palm. Scroll grips are ideal for bent shaft paddles where the blade presentation is always the same.

Choosing a paddle

You will find an enormous difference in the performance and feel between a cheap general purpose paddle and a more expensive one. The blade should be as stiff as possible, giving it a good grip in the water, with as little spillage of water from around the blade as possible. However, a little spring in the shaft will prevent jarring to your hands and joints. Lay your paddle across your palms, with the grip in one hand. Bounce the blade end up and down so that the shaft near the neck hits the heel of your hand. You will be able to feel and see the shaft quiver

after each impact if there is some flexibility.

Some blades slice edge-on through the water more easily than others, depending on the profile of the blade. Many paddle skills utilize this slicing action. The best way to assess this aspect of blade performance is to slice it around in the water. A blade that is the same thickness at the edge as it is at the centre will probably not feel as good as one that is thinner at the edge. A blade with a badly contoured stiffening rib down the centre of the blade will drag badly in the water when sliced.

Make sure that the hand grip is comfortable through the expected range of movements and that it fits your hand.

You have a choice of materials including shafts of aluminium, GRP (or carbon fibre) and wood, with a blade of wood, plastic, GRP or of sandwich construction with a metal rim. Your choice may be influenced by the 'feel' of the paddle in the water, by how much abuse you think it could take, by the materials used, by the price or by availability. Paddle choice is personal: you should like the feel and look of your paddle. But, if you are uncertain about which type to purchase initially, go for a general purpose blade that will allow you to practice the whole range of paddle skills. You will probably need a spare in the future, so when you have a better idea of what you would really like, your initial purchase can be carried as the spare.

Bent paddles with scroll grip